MOVING BEYOND ACADEMIC DISCOURSE

MOVING BEYOND ACADEMIC DISCOURSE

Composition Studies and the Public Sphere

Christian R. Weisser

With a Foreword by
Gary A. Olson

SOUTHERN ILLINOIS UNIVERSITY PRESS
Carbondale and Edwardsville

Library of Congress Cataloging-in-Publication Data

Weisser, Christian R., 1970–
    Moving beyond academic discourse : composition studies and the public sphere /
Christian R. Weisser ; with a foreword by Gary A. Olson.
        p. cm.
    Includes bibliographical references and index.
        1. English language—Rhetoric—Study and teaching—Political aspects—United
States. 2. English language—Rhetoric—Study and teaching—Social aspects—United
States. 3. Academic writing—Study and teaching—Political aspects—United States.
4. Interdisciplinary approach in education—United States. 5. Education, Higher—
Political aspects—United States. 6. United States—Intellectual life—21st century. I. Title.

PE1405.U6 W45 2002
808'.042'071—dc21
ISBN 0-8093-2416-4 (pbk. : alk. paper)   2001031155

FOR MY MOTHER,
a true believer in innate human goodness

CONTENTS

FOREWORD
PUBLIC DISCOURSE AND THE FUTURE OF
COMPOSITION PEDAGOGY

T HE CHIEF acquisitions editor of a major textbook publisher came to
Tampa recently to "consult" with me. He had been visiting a number of senior compositionists across the country with one primary mission: to discover if this group of people active in the field had a clear, consensual notion of "where
the field is heading," what new pedagogical and intellectual directions it was likely to
take. As is to be expected from any effective entrepreneur, this editor hoped to ride
the crest of the newest trends, outwitting his competitors by being the first to produce the textbooks that would reflect those trends. I tried to oblige, mentioning a few
areas that I thought promising, including visual rhetorics and post-process composition, but I saved until last the area that I thought would most likely lead us all into the
new decade: public writing, especially as it is linked to service learning. His eyes immediately lit up (I could almost see the dollar signs shining in his pupils), and he commented excitedly, "This is incredible. Practically everyone that I've consulted has said
the exact same thing."

The reason that there seemed to be such an unusually high degree of consensus
among a collection of people who otherwise would be expected to disagree about
practically everything else related to the field is that public writing is clearly emerging as a powerful expression of some of the field's most cherished values. There is,
for example, a strong recognition that the most effective writing pedagogy stresses that
all writing done in "the real world" is directed to a particular audience for a specific
purpose. Too often, composition pedagogies have been thoroughly arhetorical, direct-
ing students to write to no one for no apparent purpose ("Write a three-page paper
on abortion"). The move toward public writing is an effort to reinstate rhetoric as the
heart of effective composition pedagogy. As such, it is an implicit critique of those
pedagogies that center on teaching students to "express" their inner feelings and not
to "worry" about audience, to write principally "for one's self."

Moving Beyond Academic Discourse is certain to become a rallying point in this movement toward helping students discover forums for public discourse. Sophisticated,
insightful, and forward looking, *Moving Beyond Academic Discourse* deftly builds a case
for making public discourse central to composition pedagogy. Christian Weisser pas-

sionately argues that composition pedagogy has progressed from a preoccupation with the individual writer to a recognition of writing as a social act to an understanding of writing as a site of political and social engagement to our present concern with integrating public writing into the curriculum. In effect, he sees the move toward public writing as a natural outgrowth of the earlier Freirean liberatory pedagogy.

This book is in part a critique of the scholarship in rhetoric and composition that addresses public discourse. Weisser attempts to reinvigorate this scholarship by drawing on the work of Jürgen Habermas and Nancy Fraser in order to present a richer, more nuanced conceptualization of the public sphere—one that rejects the weak, liberal notion of a consensus-driven public and that imagines instead a site of continual contestation and constant hegemonic struggle. Thus, he challenges us all to make our students' writing experiences as authentic as possible, to go beyond the simplistic letter-to-the-editor assignments of the past. In fact, for Weisser, these considerations are intimately linked to our own roles as "public intellectuals," for it is through our own and our students' writing that we have the greatest ability to effect change in the world.

You will find *Moving Beyond Academic Discourse* to be a provocative, stimulating, well-argued, and well-written book. Christian Weisser challenges us to make the most of our roles as composition instructors and public intellectuals—and, in this book, he sets a fine example for all of us.

GARY A. OLSON

PREFACE
PUBLIC WRITING IN CONTEXT

> Most of us, despite the outrage we may feel about governmental cowardice or corruption, and despite our despair over what is being done to the weakest and poorest among us, still identify with our country. We take pride in being citizens of a self-invented, self-reforming, enduring constitutional democracy. We think of the United States as having glorious—if tarnished—national traditions.
>
> —RICHARD RORTY, *Philosophy and Social Hope*

I WANT TO begin this book with a note of praise for the many English and writing teachers—at both the secondary and postsecondary level—who work to bring greater efficacy to student writing by engaging with public audiences and issues. As many of you who are reading this already know, moving the work that we do into larger public spheres is not often easy. Involving students in "public writing" is fraught with headaches of all sorts. Carefully structured discussions and exercises become nearly impossible. Helping students find forums and situations for public discourse demands an enormous amount of time. Providing feedback to students and supervision of student activities demands nearly constant attentiveness. Merely proposing and initiating such courses can become an administrative nightmare, filled with forms, approval sheets, waivers, and other types of organizational documentation.

That is not to say, however, that writing courses that engage in public discourse are not worth the effort. In fact, it is often *because* of these obstacles that such courses are so enormously rewarding for both students and teacher. The carefully structured and sanitized discussions of the typical classroom are often replaced with animated, engaged, and at times feverishly pitched discussions about the ways that students use their discursive talents to make voices heard and bring about palpable changes in their communities. The extra time spent designing and implementing such courses is often exponentially rewarded by semester's end, when many of those involved feel that they've been a part of something worthwhile. In fact, even jumping through administrative and organizational hoops to design and implement "public writing" courses can bring us closer to our students, who stand in financial-aid lines for hours, are blocked out of required courses, and often feel incapable of making their voices heard to those in control of many aspects of their academic lives.

After a panel on service-learning at the 1999 CCCC Convention, I had a "hallway conversation" with several other writing teachers who had designed and taught public writing courses. While all of our experiences were quite different, our common impression was that we had all been through an experience that was trying—at times grueling—but also incredibly memorable and rewarding. Our conversation moved from the hallway to the lobby, then on to the dining room. As we spoke at greater length, I noticed that our discussion was replete with images and metaphors similar to those I've heard from war veterans, plane crash survivors, and team athletes. In fact, one fellow teacher envisioned public writing as being "down in the trenches." Shared experiences have the tendency to bring people closer, to cause them to develop bonds of work and friendship, and to learn together as they overcome and succeed. Adversity forms close bonds. While I'm certainly not suggesting that teaching public writing is anything like war or a plane crash, I do believe that the experiences that emerge from public writing courses have the potential to bring us closer to our students through shared work, shared successes, and occasionally, shared commiseration. Perhaps more importantly, these experiences have the potential to foster in students the ability to speak for themselves and others in larger public spheres. As you enter the trenches of public writing, I hope that this book will help you to better contextualize an issue of great importance in composition studies today: how to move writing instruction into the public sphere.

One of the theoretical points I make in this book is that effective public writing must account for the degree to which discourse exists in a historically textured sphere that is the product of countless social and political forces. In fact, I believe that successful discourse in any community recognizes the types of conversations that have preceded it, the style in which arguments are presented, how interlocutors are evaluated, and what can and cannot be said in this community. For that reason, I begin *Moving Beyond Academic Discourse* by introducing the historical background of the current discussions surrounding public discourse within composition studies. Chapter 1, "The Growth of a Discipline: Student-Centered Approaches to Writing Instruction," describes the intellectual, cultural, and academic circumstances and conditions that preceded composition's recent interest in public writing. Understanding this context is fundamental for those just entering the current conversations about writing in public spheres. This first chapter demonstrates that composition theory has gradually expanded its focus from the individual writer to social notions of how knowledge is produced to more political investigations of discourse. It proposes that the recent interest in public writing, public discourse, and public intellectualism are continuations of that very expansion.

Chapter 2, "Radical Approaches to Composition: The Writing Classroom as a Political and Public Sphere," examines more recent progressive or so-called radical theories in composition studies that consider writing as a site of political and social engagement. From these theories has emerged a body of work focusing exclusively on the efficacy of public discourse. These newest theories have recently begun to conceive of *the public sphere* as both a useful metaphor for how we might envision writing classrooms and as a site in which our students might compose more meaningful and significant work. This second chapter examines the strengths and weaknesses of this relatively new conversation in composition studies, and it concludes by introducing the work of several theorists on the public, in order to develop a fuller theoretical understanding of the topic.

Chapter 3, "Social Theory, Discourse, and the Public Sphere: New Perspectives on Civic Space," investigates existing theoretical conversations on the public sphere and considers how they are understood in contemporary social and cultural theory. The central theorist of the public is Jürgen Habermas, and his body of work—most notably *The Structural Transformation of the Public Sphere*—provides a useful starting point for nearly all discussions of the subject. Drawing from the large body of scholarship surrounding his work, I outline a fuller theory of the public for composition studies, one that envisions the public sphere as a contested, historically textured, multilayered, and sometimes contradictory site. This theory examines public discourse as a complex array of discursive practices, and it begins to extend and elucidate current conversations in rhetoric and composition concerning the public.

Chapter 4, "Rethinking Public Writing: Discourse, Civic Life, and Composition Studies," incorporates theories of the public (as outlined in chap. 3) into a more detailed critique of existing conversations in composition studies concerning the public. This chapter asks writing teachers to problematize their notions of public writing, to see public writing as more than just letters to the editor of a local newspaper or magazine, and to begin to create new definitions for writing assignments inside and outside of the classroom. Drawing specifically on the work of Nancy Fraser, this chapter attempts to dispel five primary misconceptions about the public and public discourse that persist in writing instruction. Chapter 4 concludes by presenting pedagogical directions, personal examples taken from my own writing courses, and new questions to consider for compositionists interested in public writing.

Chapter 5, "Activism in the Academy: The Compositionist as Public Intellectual," turns the discussion to the common desire among many intellectuals to have greater political and social import on public issues and conversations. By examining various perspectives on intellectualism, this chapter explores what role the intellectual has in postmodern society and to what degree the material conditions of academic life allow for public intellectualism. In addition, this chapter draws upon earlier theories of the public as addressed in chapters 2, 3, and 4 to expand upon existing notions of the public and public intellectualism and it culminates by addressing the role of the public intellectual as it relates specifically to compositionists. Overall, this concluding chapter attempts a more holistic, comprehensive analysis of the subject of public intellectualism in an effort to explain exactly how and to what degree compositionists might become more successful in their attempts to work toward a more democratic society.

One of my primary intentions in writing this book was, from the outset, to make it easily accessible to a diverse audience of theorists, scholars, teachers, and writers. In keeping with this intention, I've tried to present challenging, complex theories in a straightforward yet unmitigated manner. If our conversations about public writing are to have any real value, we must work toward connections with other disciplines, discourse communities, and individuals inside and outside of academia. Those connections might begin with the simple effort to make our own discourse more accessible to other groups and individuals. Above all else, I hope that this book is not just read and discussed by college and university English professors but is instead used and applied by writers at all levels in their efforts to speak and write in public situations. Like Richard Rorty, I take pride in being a citizen in a self-reforming constitutional democracy—despite its many inequalities. I believe that such pride is an essential component of citizenship, and I also believe that helping others to enter into public discourse is the best way to increase a democracy's vitality and strength. There is no incompatibility between patriotism and a critical desire to make our country live up to its professed ideals. Writing teachers are in a unique position to help students enter, shape, and create discursive domains where their writing takes on an important public role. Perhaps this book can provide some of the tools those students will need.

ACKNOWLEDGMENTS

Acknowledgment is an endless task; I can only begin to thank the many people who have influenced and shaped my work on this subject. First, though, I'd like to thank Gary A. Olson for his careful reading and thought-provoking questions during the earliest stages of this book. I would also like to express my gratitude to Lynn Worsham, Debra Jacobs, and Tom Ross for their helpful suggestions. I would especially like to thank Patricia Bizzell, who provided a tremendous amount of constructive feedback and support in her two reviews of this book. I owe a debt of gratitude to Sid Dobrin, Steve Brown, Julie Drew, Raul Sanchez, Joe Hardin, and Jerry Lucas for their help along the way. I owe a special thanks to Karl Kageff, acquisitions editor at Southern Illinois University Press, for his patience and suggestions over the past two years. I also thank April Komenaka, Kenny Simmons, Karla Hayashi, Luke Bailey, and my other supportive colleagues at the University of Hawaii (Hilo). Finally, I must thank Traci and Sofie, who have been there through it all; Jimmy and Jami, who kept me sane and in good spirits as I struggled to get this down on paper; and my Dad and "Big D," who invested their time, effort, and energy in my education.

MOVING BEYOND ACADEMIC DISCOURSE

THE GROWTH OF A DISCIPLINE
Student-Centered Approaches to Writing Instruction

It seems to me that the best teacher would be the one who allows students to find their way through complex material as you lay out the terrain. Of course, you can't avoid guiding because you're doing it a particular way and not some other way. But it seems to me that a cautionary flag should go up if you're doing it too much because the purpose is to enable students to figure out things for themselves, not to know this thing or to understand that thing but to understand the next thing that's going to come along; that means you've got to develop the skills to be able to critically analyze and inquire and be creative. There's sort of a classical version of this—that teaching is not a matter of pouring water into a vessel but of helping a flower to grow in its own way—and I think that's right.

    —NOAM CHOMSKY, "Language, Politics, and Composition:
A Conversation with Noam Chomsky"

WHILE OTHER composition theorists and scholars (i.e. Berlin, North, Miller) have traced composition studies' emergence and growth as a discipline, no one has looked at the move toward public writing as the most recent and most widely encompassing ramification of our discipline. While my own perception of how the field has developed might differ from that of other compositionists, I think it is fair to say that it has progressed in both scope and complexity. Since its birth as an academic discipline, composition studies has gradually expanded its focus from the individual writer, to social notions of how knowledge is generated, to more political—and public—investigations of discourse.

Growth theorists—including James Britton, John Dixon, and James Moffett—renewed interest in personal and expressive forms of talk and writing, and they focused attention on the ways that writing teachers might encourage students to use language in more complex ways. Cognitivists like Janet Emig, Linda Flower, and John Hayes extended the critique of traditional ways of teaching writing, arguing that teachers should intervene in the recursive stages of a student's writing process—a pedagogical move that would help to empower the student and transform the classroom into a more egalitarian space. Expressivists like Peter Elbow, Donald Murray, and Ken Macrorie focused attention almost exclusively on the student, arguing that truth and knowledge lie within each individual writer. While interested in responding to political and social issues, the expressivists construed discourse in individual terms. The social contructionist critique of expressivism went directly to the conception of how knowledge is generated and maintained. Social constructionist theory shifted the focus from the individual to an understanding of facts, texts, and selves as social constructs. Although social constructionist theory questioned the basis of knowledge and discourse, many compositionists felt that it did not fully inquire into the political implications of discourse: the asymmetrical power relations among different language users, and the degree to which discourse is ideological and political. As a result, progressive (or so called "radical") compositionists began to view the writing classroom as a site of social change, a place where students become their own creators of democratic culture. Although these radical theories are still very much in favor among many compositionists, some scholars have expanded the focus of these theories to explore the political role of discourse in democratic societies.

While radical theories enabled many compositionists to envision discourse as a political act, more and more scholars today are investigating the sites in which this discourse is generated and used. Many compositionists are now considering the role of discourse in political, social, and public spheres. For example, scholars have become interested in language use as it enables and inhibits participants in their struggles for public democracy and social justice. These investigations include student writers and their attempts to generate socially useful discourse, but they also include writing outside of the classroom and the role of the intellectual in constructing and maintaining public discursive spaces.

Discourse specialists in composition and English studies have recently begun to turn to scholarship outside of composition—most notably the work of cultural theorists including Jürgen Habermas, Oskar Negt, and Alexander Kluge—to inform their own discussions of the public. In composition, scholars including Joseph Harris, Susan Wells, Lester Faigley, and Irene Ward have recognized the importance of these discussions, and these scholars have incorporated some of this theoretical work into their own examinations of public writing. In English studies and sociology, theorists such as Bruce Robbins, Jim Merod, Fredric Jameson, Andrew Ross, Gerald Graff, and Stanley Aronowitz have incorporated the work of Habermas, Negt, and Kluge into their discussions of public discourse, and they have discussed the role of the intellectual in the creation and maintenance of democratic spaces. The term "public sphere" is now proliferating in titles of books, articles, and college courses. While many theorists, scholars, and educators have recognized the importance of this theoretical work to the current conversations in English and composition, no scholar has yet put forth a careful and thorough examination of the possibilities of the work of Habermas, Negt, Kluge, and others to the conversations in English-related fields. My aim, then, is to offer an in-depth exploration of these cultural theorists' work and its importance to current conversations in English studies. As more scholars turn to "the public" as a site of discursive interaction, an understanding of the work of these theorists will be of increasing importance. In order to accurately view this work through the lens of writing instruction and composition studies, it is necessary to see where we've been in order to envision where we might go.

A GROWING DISCIPLINE

While I run the risk of stating the obvious, I think it is important to note that writing instruction has been dramatically transformed in the past forty years. Its development, while fairly brief compared to many other academic disciplines, has been both progressive and ongoing. Before the 1960s, writing was seen only as a skill to be modeled and learned, and most English professors saw writing as either a preparation for practical living or as a foundation for the production of literature. Today, most composition courses are not designed solely to prepare students for the workplace, nor are they designed to emphasize the creation and analysis of literature—although they occasionally do both. Many current writing courses—and the theoretical and pedagogical discussions concerning them—attempt to prepare students for citizenship in a democracy, for assuming their political and social responsibilities, and for lives as active participants in public life.

But these goals have not always been as pronounced as they are today. The study of writing instruction—composition studies—has gone through a remarkable evolution in getting to these current goals. While it would be both foolish and inaccurate to attempt to describe anything that remotely resembles a linear history of the field, I'd like to suggest that composition studies has gone through several distinct phases, complete with leading theorists, conversations, and even particular vocabularies.

Political, social, and intellectual conditions in the 1960s and 1970s brought about fundamental changes in American higher education and composition studies. In the 1960s, language scholars began to question the product-centered notion of writing. Many writing theorists turned to intellectual inquiry and speculation about language learning that was going on in fields as varied as linguistics, anthropology, sociology, and clinical and cognitive psychology. Much of this work led writing theorists to new questions about the effectiveness of traditional, rule-bound methods of writing instruction. Noam Chomsky's work in linguistics (most notably, his *Syntactic Structures*) encouraged a new interest in the formation of language in individuals. Chomsky's notion of transformational grammar focused on the generation and development of language and asserted that the language-acquiring ability of the human mind is an innate, genetically carried attribute that is possessed by no other creature. That is, Chomsky argued that our brains are "hard-wired" for language acquisition. Francis Christensen's essays on "generative" rhetorics, which drew upon work in behavioral psychology, also stimulated interest in the process by which writers develop sentences and paragraphs. Chomsky's work, and the work of language theorists like Christensen and others, prompted writing scholars to examine the procedures by which language comes into being and scrutinize the processes writers employ to produce texts.

Because of the questions that these new theories raised, many scholars in English began to reconsider the aims and goals of the discipline. Consequently, in 1966 a group of about fifty leading teachers and scholars from America and Britain met at Dartmouth College (the Dartmouth Seminar) to discuss the new developments in language learning and attempt to define English as a subject, rethink the aims and methods of English teaching, and outline the ways it might best be taught. The plan of the seminar was to begin by bringing all of the participants together to address the question, "What is English?" It was assumed that some consensus would be formed and that the participants would then split into specialized groups to address particular issues in teaching and scholarship. The consensus that was hoped for did not occur.

The participants at the Dartmouth Seminar quickly realized that the task of defining "English" was much more difficult and complex than expected. The seminar has since been viewed as a site of conflict between British and American positions, although there were strong differences of view among the participants of each country (Harris, *A Teaching Subject* 5). The Americans, led by Albert Kitzhaber, were largely concerned with defining English as an academic discipline. Kitzhaber's aim was to form a view of English as an organized and distinct discipline with an integrity of its own. He felt that the real focus of English was as a body of knowledge to be acquired and a set of skills to be mastered. His goal for the Dartmouth Seminar was to define the parameters of the subject and identify a set of principles for use in its study. In short, Kitzhaber (and the majority of the Americans present at the seminar) argued for the need to formalize the study of English and believed that the answer to "What is English?" could be answered using the same criteria that had been used to define and identify other branches of the curriculum.

In response to Kitzhaber and the American view of English, James Britton and his British counterparts argued that the real focus of the discussion should be the development and lived experiences of students—not the justification of a discipline. Britton asserted that the questions should not be "How do we legitimize English?" but "How might the classroom allow students to use language as a means of clarifying and understanding their lives?" The British position at Dartmouth was to define English as a space in the curriculum where students might be encouraged to use language in more complex and meaningful ways. Britton suggested that students might learn how to use language more effectively through reading, writing, and talking about issues in their own lives. This approach to English—soon labeled the *growth model*—prompted a renewed interest in personal and expressive forms of talk and writing.

In general, it might be said that the American focus was on the teaching of literature while the British focus was on the responses of students to texts of various sorts—including the reading of their own lives. An excellent example of the distinction between these two views is in the way the members of each group defined their work. Ironically, the actual duties of most of the participants were very similar: most worked in university departments of English. However, the Americans defined themselves as scholars and academics, while the British thought of themselves as classroom teachers. As a result, the Americans defined English in relation to their desire to justify their work to other university professors, while the British attempted to define their work in relation to its connection to the needs and concerns of students.

These two views of English, the Americans defining it as a thing to be studied—literature, criticism, theory, rhetoric—and the British defining it much more loosely as a way of engaging with the work of the classroom and the roles of teacher and student, mark something of a turning point in English studies, particularly in composition. While this confrontation has not been resolved today—in fact, the pages of our current journals still abound with essays on disciplinary identity and attempts to define and classify English studies—the British position has had an important impact on composition theory and pedagogy.

Many Dartmouth Seminar participants were unconvinced by arguments for the growth model—American and British alike. Many feared that talk about the feelings and experiences of students would devalue the importance of English studies. However, the work of growth theorists like Britton marks a point in the conversation in which the work of the *student*—as opposed to that of the *teacher*—becomes the scene of importance. Growth theories asserted that what was most needed to make work in English more meaningful and coherent was not a more complete understanding of the structure of literature but a better understanding of how students learn to make full and expressive uses of language. This shift was one that would alter the framework of scholarly discussions about writing and literacy and would serve as the basis for conversations in composition studies in the 1970s and 1980s through cognitive, expressive, and social constructionist schools of thought. As Joseph Harris suggests in *A Teaching Subject: Composition Since 1966,* the participants at Dartmouth

> proved in fact unable to agree on much in either theory or practice, but this lack of consensus did not limit their impact on the work of many teachers then and since—for whom Dartmouth has symbolized a kind of Copernican shift from a view of English as something you *learn about* to a sense of it as something you *do.* After Dartmouth, that is, you could think of English as not simply a patchwork of literary texts, figures, and periods (Swinburne, *The Fairy Queen,* the eighteenth century) but as the study of how language in all its forms is put into use—from gossip to tragedies to advertising to the talk and writings of school children. An old model of teaching centered on the transmission of skills (composition) and knowledge (literature) gave way to a *growth model* focusing on the experiences of students and how these are shaped by language. (1)

While the impact of this seminar on its participants—who were among the most prominent scholars and teachers in English studies at the time—was great, one book in particular was responsible for bringing Dartmouth to the many educators who were unable to attend. John Dixon's *Growth Through English,* published in 1967 and reprinted twice afterward, offered his account of what happened at Dartmouth. While the book has been noted for its eloquent description of the conference, it has also been observed that Dixon's work advances a skewed perspective on what really took place—understandably so, as Dixon suggests early in his report that his aim at the seminar was to draw "such ideas as are directly relevant to my own work in class" (xi). As a result, Dixon's work focuses almost exclusively on the work of those scholars at Dartmouth who advocated examining new ways to enhance student uses of language. Growth theories, as put forth in the book, insist that the focus of English should be on *learners,* not teachers. Dixon was himself a "leading growth theorist, and his report offered less an account of what was argued at Dartmouth than a brief for a particular view of teaching" (Harris 1). Dixon made little attempt to account for the views of the Americans, and his book asserted the value and widespread commendation of growth theories for the majority of the conference participants. Whether Dixon's report is accurate or not is beside the point; the book was undeniably significant for growth theorists and can be seen as one of the important starting points in the move toward student-centered approaches to English.

Ironically enough, one of the most influential advocates of the growth model was an American: James Moffett. Moffett's 1968 *Teaching the Universe of Discourse* was influenced by his experience at Dartmouth, and its publication significantly shaped the teaching of writing in America in subsequent years. Moffett's earlier work, like Britton's, was influenced by the work of social scientists like Piaget and Vygotsky who asserted that our learning grew from an inner expressive base. The importance of the work of these social scientists to writing instruction cannot be overstated. Cognitive psychology, as championed by Piaget and Vygotsky, emphasized learning as a process and proposed that there are developmental levels of thinking—an emphasis that would have a direct impact on cognitive approaches to composition just a few years later. These psychological approaches led writing theorists like Moffett to "define language as a continuum extending from the purely external, referential, and objective, to the purely internal, expressive, and subjective" (Berlin, *Rhetoric and Reality* 163). In other words, the influence of this work was an important step in the shift away from traditional teacher-centered approaches and toward the student as the focus of composition studies. Moffett drew upon this work in cognitive psychology and applied it to the teaching of writing by arguing for a view of writing as a growth process. Moffett saw students as moving in their language development through levels of abstraction: from interior dialogue, to conversation, to correspondence, to public narrative, to published generalization and inference. The distinctions have to do with the distances separating interlocutor, audience, and subject. Moffett thus recommended writing and speaking activities that are appropriate to the stages of the student's development.

A CHANGING CLIMATE

So, the move toward student-centered approaches to the teaching of writing had been developing for some time. Named by James A. Berlin as "the Renaissance of Rhetoric," the period from 1960 to 1975 witnessed the gathering momentum of a new perspective that was to change the discipline of composition fundamentally in years to come *(Rhetoric and Reality)*. In the early 1970s, this new perspective blossomed into what many compositionists perceive as a revolution in the teaching of writing. The most widely accepted account of this revolution is the paradigm shift theory, and two versions of it have been particularly influential: Richard Young's 1978 "Paradigms and Problems: Needed Research in Rhetorical Invention" and Maxine Hairston's 1982 "The Winds of Change: Thomas Kuhn and the Revolution in the Teaching of Writing." Hairston suggests that this move or revolution in the teaching of writing illustrates Thomas Kuhn's theory of scientific revolution. Kuhn's theory posits that major changes come about as a result of breakdowns or failures in intellectual systems. These breakdowns occur when a significant number of established investigators in the field encounter problems that can't be solved using established methods. Kuhn calls the change in theory that underlies this kind of revolution a *paradigm shift*. Kuhn's work is usually identified with scientific fields, but it is easily applicable to most areas of intellectual inquiry, including English and composition studies. Hairston suggests that "we are at the point of such a paradigm shift in the teaching of writing, and that it has been brought about by a variety of developments that have taken place in the last 25 years" (14).

As the work of scholars like Christensen and growth theorists like Britton and Moffett suggests, many writing teachers were unsatisfied with the traditional teacher-centered models. The traditional paradigm, with its emphasis on the composed product rather than on the composing process, its focus on the teacher as a depositor of knowledge, and its assumption of an unchanging reality that is independent of the writer and that all writers are expected to describe in the same way, regardless of the rhetorical situation, was becoming increasingly unproductive and problematic. More and more writing teachers were discovering that the hours they spent lecturing and the late nights devoted to "bleeding" over student papers with "The Red Pen" were having little overall effect on the quality of writing their students were producing. Many writing teachers were exhausting themselves "trying to teach writing from an outmoded model, and they came to despise the job more and more because many of their students improved so little despite their time and effort" (Hairston 18).

As a result of the many questions and disappointments that the traditional paradigm raised, many writing teachers were becoming increasingly interested in pedagogical and theoretical approaches that were more directly concerned with the students' role in the classroom, as opposed to earlier models that focused on the text. Writing teachers began turning to newer student- and process-centered approaches to writing instruction. Significantly, new research in the late 1960s and early 1970s began to discount traditional methods of writing instruction and served to bolster support for new approaches. It is important to note that the traditional paradigm did not grow out of research or experimentation. It was derived partly from the classical rhetorical models of discourse, but it was primarily based on some "idealized and orderly vision of what literature scholars, whose professional focus is on the written product, seem to imagine is an efficient method of writing" (Hairston 16).

So, a paradigm shift toward process and student-centered approaches began to occur among writing teachers, researchers, and scholars. More and more evidence mounted that the old ways of teaching writing were ineffectual. Of course, these shifts in theoretical and pedagogical approaches were just the beginnings of a major paradigm shift and would probably not have brought about such immediate and drastic changes in and of themselves. A number of political, economic, and social forces were also affecting the climate of higher education in general—and college-level writing instruction in particular. Profound external forces were putting pressure on the traditional approach to teaching writing. Among the most significant of these concrete external forces were open admissions policies at many colleges and universities, the return to school of nontraditional students (many of whom were returning veterans, minorities, and women), the growing numbers of high school graduates who wished to attend college, and the huge percentage of instructors who were untrained and uninterested in teaching writing.

Open admissions policies at many colleges and universities brought millions of students—white and black, men and women, traditional and nontraditional—to writing classrooms across the nation. In the spring of 1970, for example, the City University of New York initiated an open admissions policy that brought unforeseen numbers of new students to first-year composition courses. As Mina Shaughnessy writes in *Errors and Expectations,* the new CUNY admissions policy

> guaranteed to every city resident with a high school diploma a place in one of its eighteen tuition-free colleges, thereby opening its doors not only to a larger population of students than it had ever had before . . . but to a wider range of students than any college had probably admitted or thought of admitting to its campus. (1-3)

This influx of new and diverse students was not limited to large metropolitan universities such as CUNY. Nationwide, students were enrolling in colleges, and many of these incoming students differed from the traditional white, upper-class male student of earlier decades. Between 1960 and 1980, American colleges and universities saw an increase in enrollment of 8.5 million students. Of these new students, minorities represented 17 percent and women students slightly outnumbered male students (Kerr xiv). These new students, many of them returning veterans or members of other groups of older, more experienced members of society, were less rule-bound and docile than traditional first-year students. They challenged the conventional methods of writing instruction, asked questions that were dissimilar to those asked by students who were enmeshed in traditional education systems, and in turn, compelled writing teachers and theorists to reexamine familiar classroom approaches.

These nontraditional students, as well as a greater number of traditional high school graduates going on to college, placed a new strain on already troubled methods of writing instruction. A new classroom was emerging, one which brought different perspectives and lifestyles together in what had been a fairly uniform learning environment, comprised of homogeneous students. The changed student body significantly affected writing instruction—as well as most other aspects of higher education. As Shaughnessy suggests, "academic winners and losers from the best and worst high schools in the country, the children of the lettered and the illiterate, the blue-collared, the white-collared, and the unemployed" were suddenly brought together in a system that was largely unable to accommodate such difference (3). The college classroom reflected (as it still does) a troubled version of America, a society in which cultural diversity necessitates new ways of thinking and acting. As Xin Liu Gale suggests, the modern consciousness, "when reflected in the college classroom, becomes a catalyst for change" (8). A multiplicity of cultural modes, values, and literacies were entering the college classroom, erasing not only the class basis for traditional writing instruction, but also altering the foundation of the teacher's authority and the unquestioned devotion to the text. Writing teachers operating from traditional perspectives found themselves faced with new challenges in the classroom, and they quickly discovered that traditional ways of teaching no longer sufficed.

It is significant to note that the traditional system of teaching writing was particularly vulnerable because it was staffed largely with untrained teachers who had little interest in this kind of teaching. Most English departments were almost exclusively comprised of faculty members trained and educated in literature. The growing numbers of incoming first-year students necessitated a greater number of composition courses. Large numbers of literature specialists found that they were going to be teaching a significant amount of writing in the future. For many of them, their last experience with a composition course had been their own undergraduate courses, courses that had probably been taught by other professors like them who had little or no experience, interest, or training in writing instruction. Graduate students—nearly all of whom were working toward degrees in literature—were assigned to teach composition with little or no theoretical or pedagogical training. Few graduate courses were in place to train new teaching assistants; for the most part, it was assumed that if these graduate assistants were competent writers, they would be equally competent writing instructors. As Stephen North explains in *The Making of Knowledge in Composition*,

> With very few exceptions, there were no graduate programs in Composition before the mid-1970s. Composition, described so often as the "ghetto" or the "stepchild" of English departments, was something that had to be taught—or, perhaps, endured. But it was not perceived as a discipline or field, as a subject matter suitable for graduate study. (ix)

In short, writing instruction in many universities was undervalued and often disregarded. The practitioners—those teaching a large portion of the writing courses in colleges and universities—lacked the knowledge or methods to teach effectively. Composition instructors—most of whom were untenured—were regarded by many literature faculty as second-class citizens. In the decades to follow, though, composition would begin to slough off this image, as new theories and pedagogies gave greater prominence to the status of writing instruction in American colleges and universities.

Cognitivists and the Students' Writing Process

As I hope this discussion has begun to demonstrate, significant forces were at play in writing instruction in American colleges and universities during the 1960s and 1970s. In composition studies, the so-called "current-traditional paradigm" was gradually losing its grip on composition teaching. As a result, a number of influential theories emerged to address the problems of the old paradigm. As indicated earlier, many of the important theoretical developments in composition at this time were inextricably a part of political and social activism on college campuses. New theories in composition were, in fact, involved in "a dialectical relationship with these uprisings, both shaped by them and in turn affecting their development" (Berlin, *Rhetoric and Reality* 177). The demand for relevance—specifically, making the work of the classroom relevant to the lives of students—was commonplace. Through greater attention to the role of the student—both in the classroom and in society—the new approaches to composition were attempting to respond.

Perhaps the most significant of these new approaches were cognitivism and expressivism. What is most striking about the new approaches to writing instruction at this time is that despite their many differences in both epistemology and practice, they are marked by a common and profound dedication to the student—a commitment that was much more explicit than it had been during earlier decades of writing instruction. In addition, these new approaches shared the assumption that the traditional way of teaching is inadequate and that the role the traditional teacher plays is problematic. These theories argued for greater attention to the writing that was being produced by students and less attention to the consumption of great works of literature. These new theories all shifted the focus of composition studies from the composed product to the composing process, from the teacher's monologue to the student's dialogue, and from the text as the nucleus of the writing classroom to the student as the locus of knowledge. As a result, these new approaches contributed in different ways to changing the writing classroom.

The cognitivists' major contributions to a new perception of the role of the student was in their inquiry into the process of writing and its emphasis on the teacher's intervention in the recursive stages of the student's writing process. Based on cognitive psychology, this approach suggested that both language and learning are parts of development and of cognitive stages. In other words, cognitivists asserted that learning to write requires the right experiences at the right moment. Without these experiences, or with the wrong sequence of experiences, a writer cannot mature. Cognitivists challenged the assumption that teaching writing is a mechanical act of "requiring students to imitate the master's writing and to produce their own products" (Gale 13). Rather, cognitive theories asserted that by learning about the stages a writer goes through and intervening during these stages, writing teachers might facilitate the development from one stage of writing to the next. In attempting to understand the nature of writing, the cognitivists explored the nature of these stages, how they unfold or fail to unfold in time, and how they are involved in the composing process.

One of the most significant works of cognitivism is Janet Emig's *The Composing Process of Twelfth Graders* (1971). Her monograph was the first thorough observational study of how writers go about producing texts. Before her study, as Emig is quick to note, descriptions of the writing process had been inferred from a number of well-known authors, through memoirs, interviews, drafts of published works, and from the prescriptions of rhetorics and handbooks—but never before had these descriptions been drawn from the notes of a writing scholar who had directly observed a number of writers and interviewed them about their composing process. Emig's work was a "landmark study of student-writers" that "called on some of the basic assumptions of the cognitivists" (Berlin, *Rhetoric and Reality* 159–60).

Emig's case-study approach, based in part upon Piaget's cognitive studies of language and thought in children, looked at the structural process of a group of high school seniors. Twelfth graders were chosen because "ostensibly they have experienced the widest range of composition teaching presented by our schools," and, by implication, have attained the highest levels of the developmental stages of learning and writing (3). In the summer of 1967, Emig met with eight separate students on four different occasions. In their first two meetings, Emig asked her subjects to draft a short essay while "composing aloud"—that is, while verbalizing as much of what they were thinking about as they possibly could. For their third meeting, she asked them to bring with them some writings they had done in the past—preferably in the distant past—and to draw upon these materials in discussing with her their "writing autobiographies." At their final meeting, Emig asked these students to write a short, creative text beforehand, to bring all drafts of the text with them, and to talk about how they went about composing it.

Emig's technique of "composing aloud" proved of "immediate and practical use to an entire generation of compositionists—including Donald Graves, Sharon Pianko, Sondra Perl, Nancy Sommers, Carol Berkenotter, and Linda Flower and John Hayes"

(Harris, *A Teaching Subject* 58). Emig's interest in writing as a process was quickly adopted by those who, since Dartmouth, had shifted their focus to the experiences and perspectives of the student. For example, when Donald Murray spoke in 1972 of "teaching writing as process, not product," the first three implications he listed as following from this shift in perspective had to do with a renewed focus on the student's own writing, subject, and language (91).

One of the most important features of Emig's study is that it challenged the current-traditional assumption that teaching writing is a perfunctory act wherein students observe "good writing" as demonstrated by the teacher and mimic it to produce their own good writing. These current-traditional approaches considered writing to be a mysterious process that couldn't really be analyzed or studied. Emig's work led to a new conception of writing as something with discrete stages. Moreover, she observed that the stages of writing were the same for all the students she investigated and that these stages were recursive rather than linear. That is, Emig argued that good writers employ a series of steps—broadly defined as prewriting, writing, and revising—and that these steps are often revisited during composition. Believing that there are "elements, moments, and stages within the composing process which can be distinguished and characterized in some detail," Emig called attention to new possibilities for teaching writing— possibilities that accounted for the teacher's ability to intervene in the composing process and guide students toward more effective writing (33). As James A. Berlin suggests, Emig brought about an awareness of "the effects of intervening in the developmental process as well as with the ways in which the process varies among cultures and even personality types" (*Rhetoric and Reality* 160). In emphasizing the importance for the teacher to know how students compose and why they compose the way they do, Emig decentered the traditional teacher's authority, while at the same time privileging the work and perspective of the student.

In pointing to the research implications of her study, Emig suggested that the cognitive approach equally applies to nonacademic writers and the work they produce. All successful writers, she argued, rely upon a process model of writing. Although her focus was on the writing process of a small number of twelfth graders, Emig invited research into the composing process of "persons of all ages" (5). She "recommended comparing the process and practice of her twelfth graders with that of both professional and nonprofessional adult writers" (Berlin, *Rhetoric and Reality* 160). In fact, she urged writing teachers to *be* writers and to explore the process they used in their own work. In doing so, Emig helped to expand the work of composition studies beyond the classroom to writing in a variety of private and public settings. Emig's work not only contributed to the paradigm shift toward more student-centered approaches to teaching writing, but it also helped to transform composition studies into a discipline that examines the production of texts in a greater variety of material circumstances than it had in the past.

Linda Flower and John Hayes were also important in the cognitivist movement in composition. In their important work, "A Cognitive Process Theory of Writing," they propose that writing is a goal-oriented process. Flower and Hayes based their proposition upon a greater number of observed subjects, consisting of both experienced and inexperienced writers from inside and outside of academia. Their study, which was conducted over a period of five years, led them to the observation that the mental process of writing consists of three stages: the planning stage, the translating stage, and the revising stage (372–74). During the planning stage, writers generate ideas, organize them, and set specific and general goals for the completion of their work. During the translating stage, writers put ideas into "visible language"; that is, writers transcribe their thoughts onto paper in a form that their readers might be able to understand. In the revising stage, writers evaluate what they have already written and make changes to it. What distinguishes experienced, successful writers from inexperienced writers is their ability to set "process goals" (the internal guidelines writers use to determine how they will complete the process of writing) and "content goals" (an agenda of information the writer wants to deliver to their audience). In other words, Flower and Hayes argued that successful writers have the ability to regulate, to some degree, both the steps they will go through during the composing process and the material they will use in completing a piece of writing. They suggest that this process is hierarchical; successful writers use an ordered network of goals that in turn, guide the writing process. Like Emig, Flower and Hayes called attention to the active role of the student (or writer) in producing a text. In the book's conclusion, they argue for a student-centered approach to teaching writing:

> By placing emphasis on the inventive power of the writer, who is able to explore ideas, to develop, act on, test, and regenerate his or her own goals, we are putting an important part of creativity where it belongs—in the hands of the working, thinking writer. (386)

Flower and Hayes's inquiry into the writing process of successful writers furthers the shift toward student-centered approaches to writing and also extends scholarship in composition to account for writing that is generated in nonacademic contexts. Xin Liu Gale asserts that "Flower and Hayes's study implicitly criticizes the traditional way of teaching writing, especially its emphasis on students' passive imitation of the master's great pieces" (14). Their work accentuates the importance of the student's internal processes during composition and helped to dismantle the current-traditional belief that students learn through mechanical imitation. Further, Flower and Hayes's approach affirms the teacher's responsibility to facilitate—not control or govern—the student's writing and learning process.

Janice Lauer's "Heuristics and Composition" (1970) did much to expand the focus of composition theory and research to account for work being done in other academic disciplines. As Berlin suggests, Lauer's essay was "one of the most engaging applications of cognitive psychology to composition studies" (*Rhetoric and Reality* 161). Lauer suggested that compositionists might call upon work in disciplines outside of rhetoric and English to inform their own discussions of the writing and learning process. Most specifically, Lauer suggested that work in psychology might expand many composition theorists' conceptions of invention—what Lauer assessed as the most important aspect of the composing process. According to Lauer, research in psychology might provide heuristic procedures—inventional techniques—as aids in the invention process. Lauer's work was among the most successful of the early attempts to expand the conversation in composition to theoretical inquiry in other disciplines, and it urged compositionists to explore flexible guides to the act of creation.

The cognitivist's explication of process theories allowed for a new conception of the roles of teacher and student. As Gary A. Olson suggests, the "process orientation helped us to theorize writing in more productive ways than previously and to devise pedagogies that familiarize students with the kinds of activities that writers often engage in when they write" ("Toward a Post-Process Composition" 7). Current-traditional approaches asserted that the teacher was the center of the learning equation and that the student need only imitate the "master's" prose. Cognitive approaches helped compositionists see some of the reasons for students' performance problems, and, as a result, it enabled teachers to become more involved in student writing activities.

In emphasizing the importance for the teacher to know how students compose and why they compose the way they do, the cognitive approach to composition helped to decenter the traditional teacher's authority while recognizing the student's own active role in producing a text. However, there are problems with the cognitivist approach, problems that later theories and perspectives addressed in much detail. While cognitive theories suggested that teachers should step down from their thrones as all-knowing masters and participate in students' composing processes, they kept the basic structure of the classroom intact. In their insistence on writing as problem-solving and goal-oriented activities, many cognitivists implied that the teacher's authority should be maintained because teachers have the cognitive skills to help less-experienced writers. In the cognitivist classroom, the teacher might give up the comfortable and secure place at the front of the classroom to intervene in the students' writing process, but "the traditional teacher's authority, now further secured by the claim of the scientificity and neutrality of the teacher's knowledge and problem-solving skills, remains the controlling power in the writing class" (Gale 28). Cognitivism affirmed the power of the teacher's discourse by implying that only through mastery of the teacher's way of writing will a student be able to join the ranks of the successful writer. The teacher's writing was, by definition, effective or cognitively mature, and this particular type of discourse was established as the goal for students to reach.

Cognitivists advocated the teacher's interaction with students during the writing process, but cognitivists did not question the political implications of the discourse students were supposed to master. In other words, cognitive approaches did not recognize the degree to which the social and political contexts of discourse open up or foreclose the possibilities of mastering dominant discourse for particular students. Cognitivism assumed that all cognitive development occurred independent of social and political factors. Successful writing, then, was seen by cognitivists as a "scientific fact," free of ideological factors. The possibility that what is good and successful is a product of class interest and social formations was never seriously considered. As Berlin suggests,

> That the cognitive skills leading to success may be the product of the experiences of a particular social class rather than the perfecting of inherent mental structures, skills encouraged because they serve the interests of a ruling economic elite, is never considered in the "scientific" investigation of the mind. ("Rhetoric and Ideology" 483)

Despite the many problems (which some recent work in composition has been quick to note) with this approach, cognitivism was an important step in the shift toward more student-centered—and ultimately more political and social—approaches to composition. Through its inquiry into the writing process and its assertion of the importance of teacher intervention into students' writing activities, cognitivism hastened the development of student-centered approaches in years to come.

Expressivists and Individual Knowledge

While cognitive approaches to writing instruction were abundant in the 1960s and 1970s, expressivism was perhaps the most pervasive school of thought in composition studies at the time. While there was some diversity among the theories and theorists involved in this approach, they shared a common epistemology: the belief that truth and knowledge lie within the individual writer. While interested in responding to political and social issues, the expressivists construed discourse in individual terms. As Berlin writes,

> For the expressionist, truth is always discovered within, through an internal glimpse, an examination of the private inner world. In this view the material world is only lifeless matter. The social world is even more suspect because it attempts to coerce individuals into engaging in thoughtless conformity. For the expressionist, solitary activity is always promising, group activity always dangerous. (*Rhetoric and Reality* 145)

Expressivists see reality as arising out of the private vision of the individual. They were interested in emphasizing writing as discovery—specifically, discovery of the self. In other words, expressivists saw writing as an act that authenticates and affirms the self.

While cognitivists criticized the traditional teacher's authority because it failed to facilitate students' writing processes, expressivists unequivocally objected to current-traditional approaches on the grounds that they impeded creativity—the basis for self-discovery and successful writing. Essays arguing for writing as self-expression were certainly influenced by growth theorists such as Dixon, Britton, and Moffett, but new expressivist rhetorics were equally influenced by the growing trend toward political and social activism in American society. Some expressivists criticized not only the traditional teacher's authority, but also the university and higher education itself. For example, Charles Deemer attacked the university, asserting that it stifles creativity, fragments the lived experiences of students, and alienates them from discovering their "true selves." Deemer called for the composition course to "become 'an experience' in which the teacher's authority is removed by having the student become an equal participant in learning" (Berlin, *Rhetoric and Reality* 150). In 1971, William D. Lutz offered a similar approach, suggesting that creating a successful writing environment requires breaking down the authoritarian classroom atmosphere and creating unique experiences for students. Lutz asserted that this approach ultimately calls for "the complete restructuring of the university," including the overthrow of all grading systems and of teacher authority.

As Berlin suggests, this form of expressivism represents the "more extreme form" as it was "unsparingly critical of the dominant social, political, and cultural practices of the time" ("Rhetoric and Ideology" 485). The rejection of both the institution's and the teacher's authority is at the heart of these radical expressivist approaches. Although the radicals' advocation of overthrowing all grading systems and teacher authority was "harshly criticized by the moderate wing of the expressionist camp" that eventually became dominant, the moderate expressivists nevertheless carried on the "ideological critique of the dominant culture while avoiding the overt politicizing of the classroom" (485). Like the radical expressivists, the moderates in this camp were most concerned with personal experience, self-discovery, and individualism. Thus, they viewed all forms of political, social, and economic collectivism as inherently dangerous.

Expressivist thought asserts the importance of political protest, while at the same time it suggests that resistance can only be offered by individuals, each acting alone. Political change can only be considered by individuals in individual terms; when individuals are spared the "distorting affects of a repressive social order, their privately determined truths will correspond to the privately determined truths of all others" (*Rhetoric and Reality* 486). Hence, their insistence on the shift of power from the teacher to the student. Expressivists suggest that the writing teacher should "get out of the way" to enable students to discover their own personal truths that correspond to the same universal and external laws as everyone else's truths.

A good example of this approach is Peter Elbow's *Writing Without Teachers*. In the book, Elbow contends that the traditional teacher inhibits student development because these educators too often adhere to objective academic standards of good writing. The teacher is often "too good a reader" of student writing because he or she knows too much about the subject and is indifferent to what the student has to say and because the teacher reads student work with the expectation that it will be inferior to anything he or she (the teacher) might be capable of writing. Elbow states that though a teacher

> can usually understand everything you are trying to say (perhaps even better than you understand it); nevertheless he isn't really listening to you. He usually isn't in a position where he can be genuinely affected by your words. He doesn't expect them to make a dent on him. He doesn't treat your words like real reading. He has to read them as an exercise. He can't hold himself ready to be affected unless he has an extremely rare, powerful openness. (*Writing Without Teachers* 127)

So, Elbow makes the point that the teacher often does very little to improve student writing. He seems to suggest that learning can happen without pedagogical or institutional authority. The teacherless class gives students the freedom necessary for self-development. Through interactions with other students (who are also free of institutional or pedagogical influences), writers are able to find their own privately determined truths. Thus, the "teacherless class proves the falsity of the traditional assumption that knowledge can be acquired only through the transmitter" (Gale 16).

Elbow's work is important in that it furthered the idea that the student should be the focus of the learning experience. In fact, Elbow argues that the teacher is completely unnecessary, and that the connection between an authority figure and the learning experience is relatively arbitrary. Elbow states,

> But in proposing the teacherless writing class I am trying to deny something—something that is often assumed: *the necessary connection between learning and teaching.* The teacherless writing class is a place where there is learning but no teaching. It is possible to learn something and not be taught. It is possible to be a student and not have a teacher. If the student's function is to learn and the teacher's to teach, then the student can function without a teacher, but the teacher cannot function without a student. I think teachers learn to be more *useful* when it is clearer that they are *not necessary.* The teacherless class has helped me as a teacher because it is an ideal laboratory for learning along with students and being useful to them in that way. (vii)

Expressivists like Elbow hoped to rid classrooms of the negative influences of dominant social, political, and economic factors. As Xin Liu Gale writes, no other schools are "more explicit than expressivists in arguing that truth lies deep in each individual rather than anywhere else, not in the master, of course" (17). Donald Murray, another important expressivist, suggests in *A Writer Teaches Writing* that the teacher's role is to facilitate the learning experience through response and discussion—not through lecturing and gatekeeping. Murray's approach to teaching writing is one that accommodates the student's experiences and perspectives and takes advantage of this diversity in order to "teach less" so that students can learn more. He argues that we "learn best—at least in the study of composition—when we are *not* told in the abstract what to do and then commanded to do it, but are encouraged to write and then have the opportunity to examine what we have done" (4). Murray suggests that "the writer is on a search for himself" (4). Likewise, Ken Macrorie's *Telling Writing* suggests that writing can be learned but not taught. Macrorie envisions the teacher's role in a fashion similar to Elbow and Murray: he suggests that teachers should provide an environment of facilitating activities such as editorial groups, journal writing, and rewriting workshops. Such an environment will cultivate the individual development of students, not through direct political or social confrontation, but through greater attention to the individual's private version of reality. Macrorie argues that all writers should explore "the way language works in us" (4).

Obviously, the dominant expressivist position is not overtly political; in fact, it rejects organized political and social movements as distorting influences that get in the way of privately determined truths. Berlin suggests that for the expressivists, the personal is the political. Most expressivists like Elbow, Murray, and Macrorie asserted the value of individual personal truth as corresponding with the general truth for other individuals. Berlin argues that the underlying assumption for expressivists is that "enabling individuals to arrive at self-understanding and self-expression will inevitably lead to a better social order" (*Rhetoric and Reality* 155). This move is one that was "inherently and debilitatingly divisive of political protest, suggesting that effective resistance can only be offered by individuals, each acting alone" ("Rhetoric and Ideology" 487). The individual self is hardly capable of affecting dominant political and social ideolo gies. Expressivists, then, helped to draw greater attention to the student's role in the classroom and in the formation of personal knowledge, but they inadvertently invalidated collective political, social, and public writing practices.

Social Constructionists and Communal Knowledge

While composition theory in the 1970s focused generally on the composing processes of individual writers and the development of the personal voice, scholarly investigations of discourse and composition in the 1980s began to view writing as a complex process that conveys and creates knowledge. Composition theorists and researchers began to focus on the social nature of writing and suggested that the correlation between social experience and writing ability is palpable. As I've suggested, cognitivists indirectly rejected traditional ways of teaching, arguing that teachers should intervene in students' writing practices rather than attempting to control or direct them. In effect, cognitivists called attention to the active role of a writer in producing a text, and they rejected the ideology of student incapacity that underlies current-traditional approaches. Likewise, expressivists openly advocated abandoning the traditional teacher's authority, asserting that student-centered classrooms give students the freedom necessary for self-development. Social constructionist work in composition built upon these student-centered notions and argued for a fuller understanding of how writing ability—and knowledge itself—is created and conveyed. Gale summarizes this development succinctly:

> Whereas cognitivists indirectly reject the traditional way of teaching and
> expressivists openly advocate abandoning the teacher's authority in the writing
> class, social constructionists' criticism goes directly to the foundation on which
> the teacher's authority is based—the conception of how knowledge is gener-
> ated and maintained. (17–18)

Social constructionist work in composition studies asserted that successful language users are those who have knowledge of the discourse community they are writing to. Specifically, social constructionist work in composition studies is based on the assumption that writing is primarily a social—that is, "public"—act. Social constructionists asserted that what we know about our world and ourselves is manufactured primarily through the social conventions we share with other human beings. Unlike earlier approaches to composition that focused on either the teacher as repository of knowledge or the student as generator of their own individual knowledge, social constructionists asserted the value of social interaction as a necessary ingredient in the formation of knowledge. Influenced by thinkers like Thomas Kuhn and Richard Rorty, this approach suggests that "entities we normally call reality, knowledge, thought, facts, texts, selves, and so on are constructs generated by communities of like-minded peers" (Bruffee, "Social Construction" 774).

Social constructionist perspectives came to dominate many scholarly discussions in composition studies throughout the 1980s. While many of its earliest proponents began to extend social constructionist thought in new and sophisticated ways as composition studies shifted toward this new focus, the most widely recognized and cited advocate of social constructionism in composition was Kenneth Bruffee. Bruffee argued that knowledge is not created within the individual self but is constructed by some community of knowledgeable peers and the vernacular of that community. That is, Bruffee's brand of social construction understands knowledge and the authority of knowledge as community-generated, community-maintaining symbolic acts. In "Social Construction, Language, and the Authority of Knowledge: A Bibliographical Essay" Bruffee asserts that

> social construction understands reality, knowledge, thought, facts, texts, selves, and so on as community-generated and community-maintained linguistic entities—or, more broadly speaking, symbolic entities—that define or "constitute" the communities that generate them, much as the language of the *United States Constitution,* the *Declaration of Independence,* and the "Gettysburg Address" in part constitutes the political, legal, and to some extent the cultural community of Americans. (774)

Bruffee's approach regards knowledge as social and communal in nature, and he looks especially at pedagogy, particularly the roles of student and teacher and the relationship between them that is affected by classroom procedures.

While Bruffee's approach did not gain widespread recognition until the middle 1980s, he had been concerned with the relationships between student and teacher since the early 1970s. In a 1972 article entitled "The Way Out," he argues for collaborative learning as a necessary approach to changing those classroom procedures that give the teacher all the power in the classroom. Bruffee suggests that since knowledge and learning do have social and communal dimensions, compositionists must begin to see "teaching and learning not just as activities which occur in a social context, but as activities which are themselves social in nature" (458).

Bruffee—in a fashion similar to the conversations in cognitivism and expressivism at the time—argues that the dominant pattern of behavior in the writing classroom is in "an authoritarian-individualist mode" that allows for no relationship between individual students (458). He proposes collaborative learning as a remedy to this stifling and ineffective arrangement and cites the successful efforts in this direction taking place outside of the classroom—especially in the women's liberation movement and in antiwar activism. Bruffee calls for a new arrangement in the classroom that consists of "a number of small groups more or less equal in power contending with one another" (462). This situation shifts the classroom dynamic from an authoritarian mode to one in which individuals support each other in collaborative relationships within a small group. Such an environment fosters social relationships "in which students share power and responsibility as well as information not peripherally but in the very process of learning" (462).

Bruffee did not fully work out the theoretical implications of his view until his 1985 article entitled "Collaborative Learning and the 'Conversation of Mankind.'" Still, his earlier work provided the groundwork for his social constructionist approach, and it was always based upon the idea that writing and thinking are social acts. As Berlin suggests, his

> later work makes clear . . . that Bruffee's critique of writing instruction and the alternative he proposed were from the start based on a conception of knowledge as a social construction—a dialectical interplay of investigator, discourse community, and material world, with language as the agent of mediation. (Rhetoric and Reality 176)

In the article, Bruffee suggests that collaborative writing and learning enable students to learn "normal discourse"—the discourse of academic, professional, and business communities. Bruffee asserts that writing teachers should engage students in conversation with their peers at as many points during the writing process as possible and that the writing teacher should "contrive to ensure that students' conversation about what they read and write is similar in as many ways as possible to the way we would like them to eventually read and write" (642). Collaborative learning provides a social context in which students can experience and practice the kinds of communication—through conversation and writing—that are valued by normal discourse communities.

Bruffee's work brought about important changes in composition and helped to initiate a long conversation on the social context of writing—a conversation that continues today. While I have focused upon the work of Kenneth Bruffee—his work was certainly pivotal in the growth and development of social constructionist approaches to composition in the 1970s and 1980s—he was by no means the only composition theorist interested in such approaches. In fact, there are nearly as many differences as similarities among those often grouped together under the rubric of social constructionism in composition studies. As Berlin points out, there "are indeed as many conflicts among this group as there are harmonies" ("Rhetoric and Ideology" 488). Richard Ohmann, W. Ross Winterowd, Ann Berthoff, Janice Lauer, and, more recently, John Trimbur, Lester Faigley, David Bartholomae, Greg Myers, Patricia Bizzell, and Evelyn Ashton-Jones have expanded social constructionist thought in more sophisticated directions. These theorists and others have more accurately accounted for the social and political issues that are involved in the construction of consensus than did Bruffee. In fact, many of the same scholars who have become associated with "radical" approaches to composition work from a predominantly social constructionist framework.

In the second chapter, I will address the work of those who extended the politically centered approach to social construction in more critical and ideologically attuned directions. Many of these scholars make the point that a variety of social factors—among them gender, race, ethnicity, class, and sexual orientation—influence the idealized conversational space envisioned by earlier collaborative learning and social constructionist proponents. Among the critics of early social constructionist approaches are those who look at writing as it exists outside of the classroom in what has been called "the public sphere." These scholars have recently begun to conceive of the public sphere both as a useful metaphor for how we might envision writing classrooms and as a site in which our students might compose more meaningful and significant work.

2

RADICAL APPROACHES TO COMPOSITION
The Writing Classroom as a Political and Public Sphere

> When a teacher discovers that he or she is a politician, too, the teacher
> has to ask, What kind of politics am I doing in the classroom? That is, in
> favor of whom am I being a teacher? The teacher works in favor of
> something and against something. Because of that, he or she will have
> another great question, How to be consistent in my teaching practice
> with my political choice? I cannot proclaim my liberating dream and in
> the next day be authoritarian in my relationship with the students.
>
> —PAULO FREIRE, *A Pedagogy for Liberation*

As I noted in the first chapter, composition theory developed away from personal notions of how discourse is produced and toward theories suggesting that discourse is the product of its social context. Social constructionist perspectives—as advocated by Bruffee and others—led to new understandings of the nature of discourse, positing that knowledge is a social artifact communally created and maintained. These social notions of discourse shifted the focus from the individual to an understanding of facts, texts, and selves as social constructs. The impact of these theories cannot be emphasized enough. In fact, it might even be suggested that social theories dominate most compositionists' current conceptions of how discourse is gen-erated. Social theories certainly appear to shape many of the conversations in composi-tion's major journals and conferences. For example, in the program for the 2000 Annual Con-vention of the Conference on College Composition and Communication—the primary gathering for scholars in rhetoric and composition—"Theories of the Social and Com-position" was one of the most prominent topic listings, with well over twenty concur-rent sessions listed in the category. A glance at the list of works cited in the most impor-tant books and journal articles published in composition over the past decade reveals an overwhelming number of references to social constructionist approaches. In short, social perspectives are the current dominant paradigm in rhetoric and composition.

This is not to say, however, that these social constructionist theories enjoy unquestioned and unchallenged support among compositionists today. Some of the most engaging and important scholarship in the 1990s has been done in attempts to clarify, elaborate on, and problematize early social constructionist theories of composition. Again, many of these critiques work from an inherently social constructionist perspective, and as such they hope to extend and elaborate upon early, rudimentary approaches to the subject without abandoning social constructionism altogether. These newer, more progressive approaches—commonly identified as *radical educationist* approaches to composition—attempted to more fully account for the relationship between power and discourse. Their impact has been profound. While the dominant theories in composition are still largely imbricated with social constructionist thought, these theories have been greatly influenced by newer radical approaches.

The radical educationists' critique of the traditional classroom and of traditional approaches to writing instruction that overlook the political and ideological ramifications of discourse have "contributed greatly to a new understanding of the teacher's authority in the classroom" (Gale 2). Radical educationists have attempted to change teachers from oppressive figures working for the maintenance of the status quo into critical intellectuals struggling to make society more equal and democratic. Like Bruffee, many early social constructionists seemed to ignore the politics underlying the eminent status of dominant and academic (very often the same thing) discourses. Early approaches to social construction often emphasized collaborative learning as the passport to learning the language of the academy, which is usually assumed to be the goal of college writing instruction. What they failed to acknowledge, however, is that this very discourse privileges certain language users (in this case, white, upper-class males) to the exclusion of others. The questioning of this dominant discourse—the teacher's discourse—is challenged by the so-called radicals in composition. Their inquiry into the role of the teacher's authority is not confined to discourse in the classroom but is associated with their interest in political equality and social justice in society. Xin Liu Gale offers this estimation of the radical educationists' position:

> For radical scholars and teachers, the traditional teacher's oppressive authority
> in the classroom is rooted in the oppressive power of the dominant culture and
> class; the asymmetrical power relationship between the teacher's discourse and
> students' discourses reflect the asymmetrical power relations among different
> ideologies; and the hierarchical classroom structure reflects the injustice and
> inequality in society at large. Inquiring into the relationships among language,

ideology, and power, radical theorists and teachers contend that the teacher's
authority is the product of the ideology of the dominant class's ideology and
its power. (22–23)

As a result of this position, radical compositionists advocate significant changes in both
theory and practice in writing instruction. They assert that the teacher's role should
be to transform the unequal power relations in the classroom through student empowerment. That is, radical compositionists argue for new approaches to writing instruction that develop political consciousness and critical thinking in students through
dialogic methods. Similarly, they also suggest that writing scholars and teachers should
begin to examine discourse outside of the university to more fully understand how
the composition classroom works as a microcosm of the prevailing discursive structure of a culture.

   This chapter focuses on the growth and development of these radical theories, and
it describes the recent move by some compositionists to examine discourse outside
of the writing classroom. By examining two new and important facets of radical composition—the investigation of "public writing" and the related inquiry into service-
learning in composition—this chapter will explore one of the most compelling lines
of thought in composition studies today. It begins by examining some of the most
important critiques of early social constructionist approaches to composition. Further,
it considers the work of compositionists who incorporated Paulo Freire's notions of
emancipatory learning and critical consciousness into their investigations of the political, social, and public functions of discourse. These "Freireistas," as Victor Villanueva
describes them, together with the critics of social constructionist thought and other
so-called "radical" compositionists, created the necessary preconditions for the complex and sophisticated discussions of public writing that exist at present. That is, the
current discussions of the writing classroom and public discourse are the progeny of
radical composition. The chapter concludes with a thorough investigation of where
this conversation on public writing stands today.

RADICAL COMPOSITION AS A CRITIQUE
OF SOCIAL CONSTRUCTIONISM

As Gary A. Olson notes in his Foreword to Xin Liu Gale's *Teachers, Discourses, and
Authority in the Postmodern Composition Classroom*, the "most consistent and persistent
effort to rearrange power hierarchies in the classroom derives from a group of Freire-
inspired scholar-teachers whom we associate with the terms 'radical pedagogy' or
'liberatory learning'" (viii). These scholars perceive the traditional classroom as a site

that is inherently implicated with the unequal power arrangements that permeate society at large. One of the most distinguishing features of the radical compositionist approach is its emphasis on *ideology*. Radical compositionists see discourse as deeply implicated with dominant ideology, and they see ideology as "transmitted through language practices that are always the center of conflict and contest" (Berlin, *Rhetoric and Ideology*, 478). Many radical compositionists might define the relationship between discourse and ideology as

> ideology always carries with it strong social endorsement, so that what we take to exist, to have value, and to be possible seems necessary, normal, and inevitable—in the nature of things. Ideology also, as we have seen, always includes conceptions of how power should—again, in the nature of things—be distributed in a society. Power here means political force but covers as well social forces in everyday contacts. Power is an intrinsic part of ideology, defined and reinforced by it, determining, once again, who can act and what can be accomplished. These power relationships, furthermore, are inscribed in the discursive practices of daily experience—in the ways we use language and are used (interpellated) by it in ordinary parlance. (479)

This vision of discourse as ideological and political has led to new understandings regarding the role of academic discourse and the power of what happens in the writing classroom. Radical compositionist approaches have led many in the field to view both teaching and writing as "political acts" that privilege some forms of discourse and those who are members of particular discursive communities, while silencing those (very often, students) who are not members of the dominant discursive community.

Some of these radical compositionist approaches critiqued Bruffee and other early social constructionists directly, while some followed in their wake and offered more oblique commentaries on prevailing social theories. Greg Myers was among the first of those who clearly critiqued the rhetorical appeals of Bruffee and other early social constructionists. In his 1986 *College English* article, "Reality, Consensus, and Reform in the Rhetoric of Composition Teaching," Myers criticized two significant aspects of the social constructionist argument for collaborative writing and group assignments: the appeal to the authority of consensus and the appeal to the authority of reality. Myers begins his argument by raising questions about two pedagogical moves that were (and still are) common in writing instruction: having "small groups of students collaborate on and critique each other's writing, and having case assignments based upon some actual writing situation, whether a technical proposal or an anthropology exam" (154). To explain why he finds these seemingly progressive appeals problematic, he draws upon the Marxist conception of *ideology*. While Myers was not the first to suggest that language is ideological, his essay influenced a number of radical compositionists and has been frequently cited. Myers suggested that ideology—the thoughts that structure our thinking so deeply that we take them for granted—plays an important role in maintaining the power and authority of dominant groups. He argued that while it may seem perverse to argue against the seemingly progressive appeals to consensus—which are at the heart of early social constructionist perspectives—consensus necessarily means that some interests are being silenced. As Myers suggested, the "ideas of *consensus* and *reality*, though they seem so progressive, are part of the structure of ideology" (156).

Collaborative learning proponents suggested that, through consensus, students learn how to interact with and learn from their peers. While this consensus seems to be a progressive move, "consensus, within the system as it is, must mean that some interests have been suppressed or excluded" (156). Similarly, Myers warns against the inclination toward consensus and group cooperation because it forces students to view the teacher as the depositor of knowledge, the purveyor of wisdom. He suggests that the "danger is that the teacher has merely embodied his or her authority in the more effective guise of class consensus . . . [and] any teacher who uses group discussions or projects has seen that they can, on occasion, be fierce enforcers of conformity" (159).

Bruffee suggested that writing is a communal activity, not just an "essence of meaning given by the individual to the community" (Myers, *Reality, Consensus* 166). He argued that collaborative writing and peer criticism enable students to gain a stronger sense of the degree to which the social context permeates what we know and how we know it. For Bruffee, the role of consensus in the production of knowledge is a given: it is not good or bad; it just "is." Myers, on the other hand, suggests that knowledge is defined and regulated by those who control the discourse. He critiqued Bruffee and other early social constructionists for their assumption that knowledge is outside the realm of people's social differences. Myers argues that to understand how power and ideology are implicated in the production of knowledge—particularly in educational institutions—compositionists should

> look over the list and ask who is most likely to be in a course on ethnography or elementary Chinese? Who, on the other hand, is likely to be in a course on English as a second language or on basic office skills? Who is likely to be in a basic writing course at the City University? To ask such questions is to realize that knowledge is not uniformly distributed in our society, and that it is not all of a piece. If we turn a blind eye to social factors we are likely merely to perpetuate the provision of different kinds of knowledge for the rich and poor. (167)

Myers goes on to suggest that social and economic factors shape and define how discourse communities are produced and maintained. He suggests that Bruffee saw these factors as unfortunate limitations to our thought and conversation that must be avoided as often as possible. Myers argues that he would

> see such limitations as giving structure to our thought. Ethnocentrism and economic interests are not just unfortunate habits, they are whole systems of ideas that people take for granted and use to make sense of the world. One cannot escape from one's economic interests and ethnic background, but one can try to understand how they shape one's thinking and social actions. (168)

Myers does not suggest any particularly innovative assignments to use in teaching writing. Rather, his goal is to encourage not a method but a more skeptical stance toward what happens in the composition classroom. This stance argues that compositionists must recognize the degree to which their classroom and discursive practices are part of an ideological structure that keeps people from thinking about their situation. However, Myers also asserts that writing instructors can resist this structure to some degree and can help students to criticize it as well. He argues not for a new kind of assignment, but for more skepticism about what assignments do to reproduce the structures of our society. He suggests that he has no "specific new ideas for what we should do Monday morning, but [he] follows with interest those of other radical teachers" (170). Also, Myers suggests that the kinds of authority embodied in the school are present in the rest of culture as well. The writer of an "engineering proposal, a magazine article, or even a poem, is constrained by structures as powerful as those determining the freshman composition theme" (169). While Myers suggests that though the trend toward viewing writing as a social process is a welcome corrective to the individualism of cognitivism and expressivism, we should not let our enthusiasm for this social view lead us to accept social construction as something good in itself.

John Trimbur's "Consensus, and Difference in Collaborative Learning" extends the left critique of early social constructionist thought and builds upon Myers's investigation of the wider social forces that structure the production of knowledge. Trimbur examines two important criticisms of the politics of collaborative learning in order to explore one of the key terms in collaborative learning: consensus. One line of reasoning suggests that the desire for consensus, as manifested in collaborative writing and learning, is an inherently "dangerous and potentially totalitarian practice that stifles individual voice and creativity, suppresses differences, and enforces conformity" (602). Trimbur cites several proponents of this stance who suggest that consensus is another word for "group think," that consensus can be used to justify the practices of a "crazy, totalitarian state," and that collaborative learning is another name for "peer indoctri-nation classes" (602). A second line of criticism, one that Trimbur obviously agrees with and hopes to expand, suggests that while things like selves, texts, knowledge, etc. are indeed socially constructed, social constructionist pedagogy runs the risk of lim-iting its focus to the internal workings of discourse and of overlooking the wider so-cial forces that structure the production of knowledge. Echoing Myers, Trimbur sug-gests that to understand the production and validation of knowledge, we "need to know not just how knowledge communities operate consensually but how knowledge and its means of production are distributed in an unequal, exclusionary social order and embedded in hierarchical relations of power" (603).

Trimbur begins by addressing the fear of conformity that is so emphatically voiced by the first line of criticism—the fear that collaborative learning denies differences and threatens individuality. In opposition to these critics, who feel that consensus is inher-ently dangerous, Trimbur suggests that consensus can be seen as representing the potentiality of social agency in group life—the capacity for self-organization, coop-eration, and shared decision making. That is, Trimbur sees consensus as a generative category that has the potential to enable individuals to participate actively and mean-ingfully in group life. Trimbur suggests that the fear of consensus often belies indi-vidualist notions of self as the inviolate starting point of education. The fear of con-sensus often betrays a fear of peer group influence—a fear that students will transform themselves from an aggregate of individuals (who are at the control of the authori-tarian teacher) into a participatory learning community. "In short," as Trimbur notes, "the critique of consensus in the name of individualism is baseless. Consensus does not necessarily violate the individual but instead can enable individuals to empower each other through social activity" (604).

Trimbur goes on to extend the left wing critique of early social constructionism, arguing that the issue here is not the status of the individual but the status of *exchange* between individuals. He notes that "Bruffee and his left-wing critics occupy a good deal of common ground concerning the social relationships of intellectual exchange as they are played out in the classroom" (604). For radical educators, Bruffee's work has been important because it recognizes that the classroom and the culture of teaching and learning are social texts. Both strict social constructionists and the radical left-wing critics who followed them viewed writing classrooms as part of a wider movement for participatory democracy, shared decision making, and nonauthoritarian styles of leadership and group life. However, these approaches differ in how they view discourse that doesn't affirm consensus. Following Richard Rorty, many social constructionists suggest that abnormal discourse, or as Rorty describes it, "what happens when some-one joins in the discourse who is ignorant of . . . conventions or who sets them aside," merely keeps the conversation going by adding new insights (609). According to Trimbur, this view of abnormal discourse, as defined by Rorty and perpetuated by Bruffee and other social constructionists, turns "crisis, conflict, and contradiction into homeostatic gestures whose very expression restabilizes the conversation" (Trimbur 608). That is, the social constructionist view of abnormal discourse merely reaffirms our commitment to the dominant conversation.

Trimbur argues, in accord with Myers and other radical critics of social constructionism, that a more productive stance on consensus is to look at it in terms of conflict rather than accord. They both want to interrupt the conversation to talk about the way consensus perpetuates itself, redefining it within the prevailing balance of power. Trimbur sees consensus in terms of differences and not just agreements. He argues that redefining consensus "as a matter of conflict suggests, moreover, that consensus does not so much reconcile differences through rational negotiation. Instead, such a redefinition represents consensus as a strategy that structures differences by organizing them in relation to each other" (608). In this light, abnormal discourse is not seen as a complement of normal discourse, but instead as the result of the set of power relations that organizes normal discourse: the acts of inclusion and exclusion that structure the practices of discourse communities. Trimbur suggests that abnormal discourse "refers to the relations of power that determine what falls within the current consensus and what is assigned the status of dissent" (608).

Trimbur suggests a more critical version of collaborative learning, one that distinguishes between consensus as a depoliticized, power-free practice that reproduces "business as usual" and consensus as an oppositional practice that challenges the prevailing conditions of production. He draws on Habermas's theory of *communicative action* to distinguish between the social constructionist perspective of consensus as a real world practice—"spurious" consensus—and the radical perspective of consensus as a "utopian" practice—"genuine" consensus—that intends to change the productive apparatus. According to Trimbur, Habermas defines genuine consensus not as something that actually happens, but instead as the counterfactual anticipation that agreement can be reached without coercion or systematic distortion. That is, genuine consensus, in Habermasian terms, describes the necessary precondition of the *belief* that communication can occur. As Trimbur describes it,

> consensus, for Habermas, is not, as it is for social constructionists like Bruffee, an empirical account of how discourse communities operate but a critical and normative representation of the conditions necessary for fully realized communication to occur. In Habermas's view, we should represent consensus not as the result at any given time of the prevailing conversation but rather as an

aspiration to organize the conversation according to relations to non-domina-
tion. The anticipation of consensus, that is, projects what Habermas calls an
"ideal speech situation," a utopian discursive space that distributes symmetri-
cally the opportunity speak, to initiate discourse, to question, to give reasons,
to do all those other things necessary to justify knowledge socially. (612)

From this perspective, consensus becomes the dream of conversation as a perfect dialogue, a necessary fiction of mutual recognition, and a utopian vision of the ideal discursive situation. According to Trimbur, consensus, when viewed in this way, does not
appear as the end of the conversation but instead as a means for extending and transforming it.

To view consensus as a utopian practice, one to strive for but that can never be
realized, has significant implications for collaborative learning in the writing classroom.
A utopian view of consensus allows students to be more critical of the conversation.
It encourages them to interrupt the discussion, to investigate the forces that determine
who gets to speak and what they may say, and what makes communication possible
or impossible. Trimbur believes that the utopian view of consensus abandons the ex-
pert-novice model of teaching and learning in favor of one that encourages students
to identify the "relations of power in the formation of expert judgment" (613).

Trimbur suggests that he is less interested in achieving consensus in the classroom
than he is in having students use "consensus as a critical instrument to open gaps in
the conversation through which differences may emerge" (614). Most importantly, he
wants to encourage a view of consensus as a critical tool to identify the structures of
power that determine who may speak. This, he hopes, might ultimately offer students
the utopian aspirations necessary to transform the conversation into one that is (relatively) free of the manipulations and constraints that are placed on participants.

Trimbur argues for a "rhetoric of dissensus" where students can learn to agree to
disagree, not "because 'everyone has their own opinion,' but because justice demands
that we recognize the inexhaustibility of difference and that we organize the conditions in which we live and work accordingly" (615). Trimbur's careful analysis is significant in a number of ways. He extends the radical critique of social constructionism
in more complex and sophisticated ways, showing the importance of the work of early
social constructionists in composition studies while advancing a more nuanced view
of collaboration and consensus. Also, he draws on the work of Jürgen Habermas—a
social theorist who, as I will show, has become more and more important as the conversations in rhetoric and composition have turned toward more direct investigations
of the political, social, and public uses of discourse. Additionally, Trimbur's notions

of dissensus and his extension of the left critique of social constructionist perspectives have been instrumental for many compositionists over the past ten years.

More recently, Evelyn Ashton-Jones extended this critique of early social constructionist theories by examining the role of gender in collaboration and group conversations. Ashton-Jones's "Conversation, Collaboration, and the Politics of Gender" is part of the radical compositionists' investigation of the ways in which political and social factors—most notably, race, class, and gender—affect discursive situations. In her investigation of gender differences and their influence on discourse, Ashton-Jones suggests that women and men are consigned, by virtue of gender, to gender-specific interactive styles, their option foreclosed in advance of any conversational encounter.

Echoing Trimbur's earlier critique of social constructionist theory, Ashton-Jones notes the wide-ranging views on the issue of consensus in collaborative learning. Despite the fact that she agrees with his leftist perspective on consensus, Ashton-Jones notes that Trimbur has not fully acknowledged the degree to which some voices are marginalized or excluded from discursive situations. She argues that while Trimbur's emphasis on power, on difference, and on a transformable reality goes far toward answering leftist objections to Bruffee's notion of consensus, Trimbur assumes that those speaking from marginalized perspectives will still have *access* to the conversation. She suggests that

> this revised notion of consensus works from a fundamental assumption that Trimbur doesn't directly address: that those speaking from marginalized and "different" perspectives—be they of race, ethnicity, gender, class, age, sexual orientation, or occupation—will, in fact, have access to the conversation, and, further, that the dynamics of the conversation itself will remain unaffected by a given participant's "difference." (6)

Ashton-Jones goes on to assert that this assumption is a false one, that many perspectives and voices often go unheard, and that, in fact, within the classroom, many perspectives will not be heard simply because the students who would or could voice them are not present.

Ashton-Jones notes that social factors—and she uses gender differences as just one example—often radically influence the dynamics of the conversation itself, determining whether and how a given "voice" is heard and interpreted. Prior to this article, most feminist work in composition that focused on collaboration did so in order to show its compatibility and affinity to feminist principles. Ashton-Jones argues that most feminist commentary, particularly in composition, had not subjected collaborative learning to the kind of scrutiny that would show it to be as problematic to women students as other more traditional pedagogies. To make her point, she briefly surveys the perspectives of feminist collaborative learning advocates and challenges them in light of several important studies of conversational dynamics between women and men.

She notes several scholars—including Cynthia L. Caywood, Gillian R. Overing, and Pamela J. Annas—who argue that there are integral and fundamental relations between feminism and collaborative writing. Ashton-Jones suggests why this connection seems to exist:

> Although some might question such fundamental links between collaborative learning and early feminism, the impetus behind the correlation is clear. Claiming for feminism such values as cooperation, connection, and validation and linking these values to collaborative pedagogies effectively establishes a binary opposition that frames feminism and collaborative learning in contradistinction to "patriarchal" values: competition, specialization, hierarchy, and more traditional, presentational pedagogies. (8)

The point she makes here is that collaborative learning has been seen as a boon to female students, who have struggled in the traditional androcentric teaching environments that pervaded (and still do, to some extent) the academy. Unfortunately, this belief, which assumes an absence of patriarchal authority in groups, fails to recognize one obvious point: even if "one construes the teacher-student hierarchy as essentially patriarchal, there is nothing here to suggest that other classroom structures are not" (10). That is, removing the traditional male-centered pedagogy from the classroom does not effectively remove all traces of patriarchy. The feminist valorization of collaborative learning, then, does not acknowledge the role gender plays in conversational dynamics.

Ashton-Jones notes a number of studies that show that gender is a powerfully operative variable in the dynamics of conversation and that inequality is indeed present in collaborative learning pedagogies—contrary to what many of its proponents would like to think. For example, Pamela Fishman observes that conversation does not just happen but is a complex, rule-bound activity that requires "interactional work" on the part of all participants. According to Ashton-Jones, Fishman's study notes that women "ask more questions (including more tag questions) and more often use hedges and 'attention beginnings'" (11). Similarly, Don H. Zimmerman and Candace West found that participants in same-sex conversations interrupted each other equally, whereas nearly all of the interruptions in mixed-sex conversations were initiated by males (14). Ashton-Jones also notes a study of mixed-sex conversations conducted by Helena Leet-

Pellegrini that shows that, even when women hold a position of power over men, women are still interrupted more often. Ashton-Jones suggests that these studies prove that conversational dynamics are largely controlled by the ideology of gender, and these conversational events are no less distinct in group writing situations. "On the contrary," she notes, "it is more likely that in writing groups women's and men's behavior will parallel the conversational events described in these studies, men interacting as the individualists pressing to get across their point of view—thus controlling the realities produced in these writing communities—and women shouldering the major share of the necessary interactional work" (16).

Why are these studies significant? They prove that gender-linked behavioral patterns in conversation will severely curtail for women the possibilities for intellectual and social development. Despite their efforts to join the conversation, women will not receive the full benefit of support from all participants. Collaborative learning groups provide simply one more example of a site where "gender-based patterns of dominance and subordination are reproduced, yet another stage on which the ideology of gender is played out in an almost ritualistic series of gender performances, males acting out what it means to be male in relation to females, and females acting out their supporting role" (17). For communicative situations such as the conversation of writing groups, this means that gender-specific power differences cannot be disregarded. Ashton-Jones's point is to raise the awareness of compositionists who endorse collaborative learning approaches to writing. Collaborative writing proponents ought not assume that in writing-group conversations men and women interact in identical or equal ways. Ashton-Jones concludes with an important reflection: although her article focuses exclusively on gender, compositionists must recognize the degree to which a number of other social factors—among them race, ethnicity, sexual orientation, age, occupation, class—influence the idealized conversational space envisioned by collaborative learning proponents.

This recognition of the effects of various social and political factors on communicative interaction has important ramifications for scholars today who are interested in exploring the discursive situations that transpire in various locations of "public" writing. Ashton-Jones notes that the sort of "participatory and democratic practices" that are examined by Trimbur in his critique of Habermas may be "neither participatory nor democratic for women" (19). She mentions a social theorist whose work will become more and more important as the conversation in composition turns more directly toward public writing: Nancy Fraser. According to Ashton-Jones, the "centrality of democratic practices to Trimbur's argument and his close attention to Jürgen Habermas both call for closer examination, an effort facilitated by Nancy Fraser's critique of Habermas" (19). Fraser reconstructs Habermas's critical social theory, noting

that his model of communicative interaction reinforces a patriarchal division between public and private spheres because it conceals the fact that women are oppressed
in both. Perhaps most importantly, Ashton-Jones notes Fraser's criticism of the
Habermasian definition of the "citizen" as one who "not only has free access to public discourse but also participates in and helps shape it" (19). This definition fails to
recognize the degree to which gender structures the roles of the participants in any
communicative situation. It depends upon the ability to participate on par with others in a dialogue—an ability that is often withheld from women.

Ashton-Jones also notes Fraser's criticism of Habermas on the grounds that while
he connects the role of the citizen to state and public spheres, he does not recognize
how the concept of the citizen is a masculine concept. She cites an important passage
in Fraser's *Unruly Practices: Power, Discourse, and Gender in Contemporary Social Theory*,
a passage that elaborates on the connections that Habermas makes among his spheres:

> And in every case the links are forged in the medium of masculine gender
> identity rather than, as Habermas has it, in the medium of gender-neutral
> power. Or if the medium of exchange here is power, then the power in
> question is masculine power: it is power as the expression of masculinity.
>   . . . Because his model is blind to the significance and operation of gender, it
> is bound to miss important features of the arrangements he wants to under-
> stand. By omitting any mention of the childrearer role and by failing to
> thematize the gender subtext underlying the roles of worker [masculine] and
> consumer [feminine], Habermas fails to understand precisely how the capitalist
> workplace is linked to the modern restricted male-headed nuclear family.
> Similarly, by failing to thematize the masculine subtext of the citizen role, he
> misses the full meaning of the way the state is linked to the public sphere of
> political speech. . . . He misses, too, the way the masculine citizen-speaker role
> links the state and the public sphere not only to each other but also to the
> family and the official economy—that is, the way the assumptions of man's
> capacity to speak and consent and woman's comparative incapacity run
> through all of them. (20)

Ashton-Jones obviously sees the importance of social theorists for composition. Her
article extends the conversations on consensus in more complex and insightful directions than those of earlier critics of social construction. When viewed as part of an
ongoing conversation, the work of Myers, Trimbur, Ashton-Jones, and other critics of
social construction paved the way for the current focus on the public and political uses
of discourse. Myers's work was among the first to see the ideas of consensus and re-

ality as part of the structure of ideology. By investigating the role of consensus in the production of knowledge, he raised our awareness of the ways that ideology is reproduced in collaborative situations, urging compositionists to recognize that while our courses are a part of an ideological structure, we can also resist this structure and help students to criticize it. Trimbur, in turn, extended Myers's leftist critique, revising the notion of consensus as a step toward developing a more critical practice of collaborative learning. He argued that consensus need not result in accommodation and can be a powerful instrument for students to explore differences, to identify the systems of authority that organize these differences, and to transform the relations of power that determine who may speak. Ashton-Jones's critique of social constructionist perspectives built upon Trimbur's revised notion of consensus, arguing that the preexisting social factors of the various participants plays an important role in determining who has access to the conversation. Taken together, these contributions to the "radical" conversation in composition studies provided much of the necessary theoretical framework for the investigations of "public" discourse that are so prevalent today.

THE FREIREISTAS

According to Xin Liu Gale, radical pedagogy in composition studies "owes its greatest debt to Paulo Freire, whose education theory and pedagogic practice have continuously inspired the radical scholars and teachers in the past three decades" (24). In fact, it could be argued that his work—most notably in *The Pedagogy of the Oppressed* (1970) and *Education for Critical Consciousness* (1973)—is directly responsible for the discipline's current focus upon public writing. Freire envisioned education as an integral part of a democracy, and he suggested that a society cannot be truly egalitarian until education becomes a practice of freedom. In other words, the connections between public discourse, civic action, and the educational systems of a society are inextricably bound up in each other. He suggested that classrooms usually model the power relations currently in force in a society. While he was describing the political and educational systems in his own country (Brazil) in much of his work, Freire's message was readily applied to the educational and political structures in the United States. The situation that pertains in the traditional classroom, according to Freire, can best be understood through the analogy of banking. In *Pedagogy of the Oppressed* he writes:

> In the banking concept of education, knowledge is a gift bestowed by those
> who consider themselves knowledgeable upon those whom they consider to
> know nothing. . . . Education thus becomes an act of depositing, in which the
> students are the depositories and the teacher is the depositor. Instead of

communicating, the teacher issues communiqués and makes deposits which the students patiently receive, memorize, and repeat. (58)

Such a system entails oppression, Freire argues, because it projects an "absolute ignorance onto others, a characteristic of the ideology of oppression," it "negates education and knowledge as processes of inquiry," and it assumes the teacher's authority over the student is natural and justifiable (58).

As a counter to the banking method of education, Freire advocated dialogic methods in education as a means to critical consciousness because they require a mutual relationship between persons. In the classroom, this means that teachers and students should be engaged with a subject in a joint search where both act as equal participants in the quest for knowledge. Mutual dialogue—as opposed to the teacher's monologue—is the means to both a more egalitarian relationship between the teacher and the student and to a more democratic and emancipatory education. Only dialogue, which requires critical thinking, is capable of generating critical thinkers. Without dialogue, there can be no communication, and without communication, real education cannot take place. This pedagogy requires a new type of thinking on the part of the teacher, a pedagogical stance wherein the teacher strives to work *with* the students—not *for* or *about* them. Freire explains:

> For the dialogical, problem-posing teacher-student, the program content of education is neither a gift nor an imposition—a bit of information to be deposited in the students—but rather the organized, systemized, and developed "re-presentation" to individuals of the things about which they want to know more. (82)

What makes the dialogic relationship possible in the interaction between teacher and student is the "reality to be transformed by them together with other men—not other men themselves" (83). In other words, the teacher and student work together, through discourse, to recognize and change the social conditions that prevent people from realizing their full humanity. The teacher's object of action should not be the student; rather, the teacher should work *with* the student *upon* the inequalities of society. As Gale argues, Freire is "never tired of emphasizing that, only when education is committed to transforming reality through investigation, only when the teacher is committed to working with students through dialogue, will education become authentically liberating and the teacher authentically humanistic and revolutionary" (25).

Perhaps the most significant aspect of Freire's educational philosophy to the current discussion of public writing is his notion of *critical consciousness* as a force for social change. Perhaps more than any other approach or perspective, critical consciousness, which Freire defines as "the capacity to adapt oneself to reality *plus* the critical capacity to make choices and to transform that reality," is the core of pedagogy and theory about public writing (*Education* 5). Most educators who involve their students in public writing assignments and courses do so with the hope that students will emerge from the semester's work with the ability to participate in critical and reformative public discourse. In other words, the goal of most courses in public writing is not just to facilitate students interactions with a specific sphere or issue, but to help students *transform* themselves into active, critical participants in democratic society.

Freire's view of education as a site of political and social struggle has certainly won the support of many scholars and teachers in the United States—including a number of scholars in English and composition studies. C. H. Knoblauch argues that *Pedagogy of the Oppressed* has attained, by "the standards of academic publishing, an iconic stature—cited everywhere, whether read or not, because hearsay knowledge alone authorizes reference to it as a germinal argument for 'critical' literacy" (50). Knoblauch emphasizes the features Freire has found in the classrooms of Brazil:

- The teacher teaches and the students are taught.
- The teacher knows everything and the students know nothing.
- The teacher thinks and the students are thought about.
- The teacher talks and the students listen.
- The teacher disciplines and the students are disciplined.
- The teacher chooses and enforces his choice, and the students comply.
- The teacher acts and the students have the illusion of acting through the action of the teacher.
- The teacher chooses the program content, and the students (who were not consulted) adapt to it.
- The teacher confuses the authority of knowledge with his own professional authority, which he sets in opposition to the freedom of the students.
- The teacher is the subject of the learning process, while the pupils are mere objects. (46–47)

Knoblauch stresses that this agenda offers everything we ought to fear in a country that claims to venerate freedom—and many of these qualities are found in the educational establishment here in the United States. He asserts that Freire's views on education have much to offer to composition studies. Knoblauch argues that a Freirean approach is unique in that it contains at its center "an enduring faith in the power of the word—as differentiated, active meaning—to transform speaking subjects and the worlds they speak" (54).

One of the most influential proponents of Freirean theory over the past twenty years has been Ira Shor. Shor underscores the importance of the dialogic method and liberatory learning in the United States in *Critical Teaching and Everyday Life*. He argues for a new approach to liberatory learning by proposing the "withering away of the teacher." Shor suggests that the teacher is expendable and should, after working as a "change agent" in the classroom, dissolve his or her authority in order to allow students to emerge with a "critical consciousness" (98). Shor views the classroom as a site where students can reflect on issues and ideas that transpire in the political and social spheres they come in contact with in daily life. He suggests that in a classroom in which the teacher has "withered away," students are able to form a critical dialogue about the "structure of social relations inside and outside their minds" (99). As students become more critical and liberated, the teacher's role changes accordingly from the "teacher/initiator" to a "peer discussant, a member of the dialogue on equal terms with all the others in the class" (101). For Shor, the "withering away of the teacher" aims to empower students by gradually strengthening their subject position and weakening the teacher's authority in the teaching process. Shor suggests that the classroom can be a powerful site in the formation of democratic practices, through both the subject matter—the student's lived experiences—and the pedagogical stance the teacher assumes.

In "What Is the 'Dialogical Method' of Teaching?" (coauthored with Shor) Freire argues that educators must not assume liberating dialogue as a mere technique to improve student outcomes. Instead, he argues, we must see the dialogic method as a means for allowing students to more fully realize their own humanity. Freire suggests that "dialogue is a kind of necessary posture to the extent that humans have become more and more critically communicative beings" (13). He feels that dialogue is a moment during which humans meet to reflect on their own reality—both inside and outside of the classroom—as they make and remake it. To the extent that we are "communicative beings who communicate to each other . . . we become more able to transform our reality" (13). Seen in this light, dialogue becomes more than just a tool for expressing thoughts and ideas about the social and political worlds we live in; it becomes, in fact, a conduit through which political and social realities are shaped and transformed. Freire suggests that this sort of critical development in students is a step toward a greater change in society, a transformation that is "absolutely fundamental for the radical transformation of society" (23). Obviously, Freire viewed education as an act through which students become more politically and socially empowered.

In a related *College English* article, Jane Tompkins emphasizes the degree to which the Freirean model of education has become an important focal point for teachers and scholars in English and composition studies. While this piece is neither long nor theoretically groundbreaking, it has nonetheless been discussed and cited often in the ten years since its publication. She asserts the need for writing and literature teachers to adopt the dialogic method of teaching advocated by Freire, suggesting that professors of English often argue for political and social change, in one way or another, but rarely institute these values in the classroom. She suggests that "our practice in the classroom doesn't often come very close to instantiating the values we preach" (653). Tompkins cites Freire's *Pedagogy of the Oppressed* as the impetus for her recognition of the distance between what we do as teachers and what we say we believe in. She argues that we need to follow Freire's advice in the book, whose "great theme is that you cannot have a revolution unless education becomes a practice of freedom" (653).

Tompkins suggests that traditional methods of instruction, which she had, until recently, mimicked without interrogation, fail to address what students might want or need in an education; instead, the old methods often focus on three things: (a) showing students how smart the instructor is, (b) showing them how knowledgeable the instructor is, and (c) showing them how well-prepared the instructor is for class. Tompkins argues that part of the reason for this unproductive approach to teaching is that pedagogy is rarely talked about by English professors, and, when it is, it is described as "the lowest of the low" and "beyond the pale." But Tompkins sees a ray of hope in this otherwise dismal pedagogical setting, for more and more educators are adopting liberatory approaches to teaching. She writes:

> But there is one thing people do sometimes talk about in relation to teaching, and they do this now more frequently than in the past. They talk about using teaching as a vehicle for social change. We tell ourselves that we need to teach our students to think critically so that they can detect the manipulations of advertising, analyze the fallacious rhetoric of politicians, expose the ideology of popular TV shows, resist the stereotypes of class, race, and gender; or depending on where you're coming from, hold the line against secular humanism and stop cannon-busting before it goes too far. (656)

Tompkins, in effect, is arguing for this new perspective of the classroom as a site for political and social change. We must, she suggests, make sure that the *way* we teach is in accord with *what* we want our students to learn. Tompkins seems to be arguing for a conception of the classroom as a training ground for the intellectual engagements students will soon face in society. Indeed, she mentions that she has "come to realize that the classroom is a microcosm of the world; it is the chance we have to practice whatever ideals we may cherish" (656). She goes on to argue that "what we do in the classroom is our politics" and that "the politics of the classroom begins with the teacher's treatment of and regard for him or her self" (660).

WRITING IN THE PUBLIC SPHERE

As I have suggested, the history of composition studies is one that has been filled with a multitude of voices, each one extending, analyzing, or critiquing those that came before it. Most of the important contributions to composition studies have built upon what has come before and contributed in some way to what has come after. That is, far from being the result of a few unique and original perspectives on writing theory and pedagogy, composition studies can be more accurately described as an ongoing conversation. Scholars add to the conversation and often steer it in new directions, but rarely do they change the framework of the discussion or the questions that the conversation seeks to answer. The participants in this conversation often have dissenting views and perspectives on particular issues, but the topics they address usually have a similar goal in mind. While it would be inaccurate to describe this ongoing conversation as consisting of distinct "schools of thought" or "camps" as some have characterized them, particular shared perspectives have affected the direction the discussion takes.

As I've suggested, since its growth and development as an academic discipline in the 1960s and 1970s, composition gradually expanded its focus from the individual writer, to social notions of how knowledge is generated, to more political—and public—investigations of discourse. Radical scholars and teachers in the field of composition have changed our conceptions of the role of discourse in shaping society. Viewing the work of composition as a democratic enterprise, some scholars have recently expanded the focus of radical investigations to explore the political role of discourse outside of the classroom. That is, while radical theories enabled many compositionists to envision discourse as a political act, more and more scholars today are broadening this notion to investigate sites outside of the classroom in which this discourse is generated and used. This investigation, which seems to fall into several related categories, including "public writing" and "service-learning in composition," might very well become the next dominant focal point around which the teaching of college writing is theorized and imagined. The proliferation of articles, chapters, and books regarding this subject seems to suggest that more and more scholars are looking beyond the classroom in their investigations of discourse.

In *A Teaching Subject,* Joseph Harris suggests that composition studies, which he describes as a "loose set of practices, concerns, issues, and problems having to do with how writing gets taught," can be traced by looking at a series of key words that have figured in the conversation (x). Harris believes that in tracking the meanings of these key words, which he defines as *growth, voice, process, error, and community,* he can make a case for composition as a *teaching subject,* as that part of English studies that defines itself through an interest in the work students and teachers do together. I'd like to suggest that we might extend this investigation to examine a new key word in the teaching of college writing: *public.* For many compositionists, the classroom—or, more specifically, the writing course—has emerged as a microcosm of the public sphere, as our point of contact with the "real" world out there somewhere. This point of contact is something that distinguishes composition from many other academic disciplines; our close and personal connections with students differentiates our work from the "merely academic" pursuits of our colleagues down the hall. If we believe that power is entrenched in discourse and that language is an instrumental tool in shaping knowledge and reality, we could, by extension, assume that the work that we do can have real implications in the world. While the question of what "public discourse" might entail has interested many, there has been little consensus on how we might answer it. Some scholars use the term "public" as a metaphor for how we might envision what takes place in the classroom. A few compositionists use the term more literally, suggesting that discourse as it exists outside of the classroom is an important area of investigation. Some have explored ways to facilitate the transitions for students from academic discourse to the type of discourse they might use in the "real world," while others have attempted to incorporate writing assignments that rely upon negotiation and contact with others in the public sphere. Regardless of their particular perspectives on what this term might mean to them and their students, public notions of discourse have become increasingly significant and compelling for a number of theorists, scholars, and teachers working in composition studies today.

While investigations of public discourse in composition studies have emerged only within the past few years, there have been rumblings in this direction for some time. One important early example of work in composition that investigates the idea of the public is S. Michael Halloran's "Rhetoric in the American College Curriculum: The Decline of Public Discourse." In keeping with other critics of current-traditional rhetoric, Halloran suggests that there is an important deficiency in the product-oriented, teacher-centered approach to discourse that had until recently dominated college writing courses. Unlike others, however, Halloran suggests that the recent revival of rhetoric has failed to adequately address this shortcoming. As the title of his article suggests, this deficiency "has to do with something [Halloran] calls public discourse" (245).

Halloran suggests that in order to arrive at a better understanding of what we mean by rhetoric, we must first distinguish between current-traditional rhetoric and the rhetorical tradition. Halloran notes that when writing teachers adopted current-traditional notions of rhetoric, which eclipsed the rhetorical tradition in the nineteenth century, they lost something of real value in the process: the focus on public discourse. He describes the rhetorical tradition as portraying

> the orator as a person who embodies all that is best in a culture and brings it to bear on public problems through eloquent discourse. Quintilian wrote of the good man speaking; Cicero of the *doctus orator,* the learned speaker. Both of them referred to a civic leader who understood all the values of his culture and used artful speech to make those values effective in the arena of public affairs. The purpose of education in the rhetorical tradition was to prepare such leaders. (246)

He suggests that the rhetorical tradition, then, gives primary emphasis to communication on public problems, problems that "arise from our life in political communities" (246). Rhetoric in the sense of an art of public discourse flourished in American colleges of the eighteenth century, but it died out during the nineteenth century. Halloran goes on to argue that the revival of rhetoric in the field of composition has failed to address the need for a revival of public discourse.

He goes on further to call attention to the history of rhetoric in American colleges, postulating that in the eighteenth century, the full classical idea of rhetoric was central to the college curriculum at universities such as Harvard, Yale, and Princeton. He suggests that there are two reasons for this emphasis: first, rhetoric was understood as the art through which all other arts could become more effective; second, oral communication was a primary pedagogical component in universities at this time. The oral component of the curriculum was public in two senses. First, it dealt with political and social problems; rarely were the topics of discussion limited to subjective or local matters. The second sense in which oration in eighteenth century colleges was public had to do with audience; as a student advanced through his four years of college, he was required to deliver public addresses to larger and larger gatherings of peers and teachers.

The point Halloran makes through this history is that rhetoric at American colleges in the eighteenth century consisted almost primarily of oral public discourse. It "stood very near if not precisely at the center of pedagogical concern" (257). It provided students with experience in public discourse and with a "tacit set of values bearing directly on the use of language in managing public affairs" (257). However, early into the nineteenth century, rhetoric in American colleges adopted many of the concerns we characterize as current-traditional—the emphasis on the written product rather than the process of composition or of communication; classification of discourse into at least four "modes" (description, narration, exposition, argumentation); concentration on correctness of usage and certain stylistic qualities—without much reference to the invention or substance of discourse.

While research into the composing process, according to Halloran, has recovered the "ancient idea of rhetoric as an art, an imprecise but still enormously helpful methodizing of a task," this new research has failed to recover the rhetorical focus on public discourse (263). Rhetoric, then, is defined not just by its theory, but by the sorts of rhetorical problems it gives rise to. The rhetorical tradition gave primary emphasis to public discourse; it was in essence a rhetoric of citizenship. Newer rhetorical forms address the role of student discourse in two primary ways: as either academic or personal. These new rhetorical forms do not, as Halloran suggests, address students as political beings, as "members of a body politic in which they have a responsibility to form judgments and influence the judgments of others on public issues" (263). Noting the relative lack of public discourse in society in the 1980s, Halloran suggests a direct link between this deficit and the lack of attention to public discourse in American colleges and universities at the time. He concludes by urging compositionists to explore the rhetorical tradition as an avenue to more public discourse. Halloran writes that as rhetorical studies begin to regain some of their "antique vitality and prominence, we might well turn some of our attention to the discourse of public life" (264).

In *Fragments of Rationality: Postmodernity and the Subject of Composition*, Lester Faigley convincingly argues for a reorientation to public discourse. He suggests that the emancipatory impulses that were prevalent at the beginning of the process movement in the 1960s and early 1970s have waned, but the new political awareness in composition studies has the potential to "recover a lost tradition of rhetoric in public life" (71). Faigley joins Halloran in his call to "reintroduce rhetoric as a means of fostering public discourse," arguing that rhetoric in the classical tradition occupied a central place in the American college curriculum in earlier ages. However, Faigley notes, we should not hope to go back to a "golden age of rhetoric," as American colleges in the seventeenth and eighteenth centuries educated only the male ruling elite. Today over 60 percent of high school graduates undertake some form of postsecondary education. This ever-increasing number of students should make us realize the possibilities available for initiating public discourse. Faigley proposes a cultural studies approach to investigating the structures of the classroom, an inquiry he feels is necessary before we can truly examine discourse outside of the classroom. Faigley suggests that

> proponents of a cultural studies curriculum . . . argue that it challenges the trend toward making exclusion the basis of education and defining higher education as the acquisition of narrowly specialized knowledge. They maintain

that rather than setting out a content to be learned, a cultural studies curriculum explores the relations among cultural practices and the political interests
of discourses. At the same time, however, the goal of reintroducing possibilities of public discourse through questioning the status quo makes the implementation of such a curriculum often difficult. (73)

Faigley advocates the interrogation of our current educational system as a necessary
precursor for an effective pedagogy of public discourse. While recognizing the difficulty of instituting public discursive practices in an educational system that seems to
deny difference and suppress meaningful discursive interaction, Faigley nonetheless
asserts that public discourse is possible and worth striving for in a writing course.
Unfortunately, his argument stops there and does not theorize as to how we might
enter or construct public discursive spaces.

Both Halloran's article and Faigley's book have been cited often in more recent
discussions of public discourse, and their charge to turn our attention to public discourse has been taken up with enthusiasm by a number of influential scholars and
theorists in composition. Perhaps the most substantial and notable investigation to
follow has been Susan Wells's "Rogue Cops and Health Care: What Do We Want from
Public Writing?" Wells uses an example of police brutality on her campus—and a
student's written response to it—to begin to address the question in her title. She describes how Arthur Colbert, a Temple University student, was stopped by two police
officers late one evening, questioned, beaten, and imprisoned for allegedly running a
crack house. After being released the next morning, the student returned to headquar-
ters and filled out a "Citizen's Complaint" form, writing three pages. The subsequent
investigation led to charges, suspensions, transfers, and other reforms. Wells writes:

> As a teacher, I was upset that a student had been brutalized. But as a writing
> teacher, I was triumphant. Colbert had probably learned to write strong
> narrative in *our* program; his complaint sounded like a successful basic writing
> assignment—good sequential order, lots of detail and elaboration, a clear,
> supportable conclusion. Someone had done good work with this student. And
> his text had been efficacious: it had turned around a whole police department,
> delivered innocent grandmothers from unjust imprisonment, and set aside
> scores of false convictions. (326)

This incident led Wells to examine our discipline's desire for efficacious public
writing—especially as it is invested in our students. Wells notes that many compositionists want to help their students to use discourse in more public ways, suggesting

that this desire imagines them in "a public role, imagining a public space they could enter" (326). Such a space, she argues, needs to be built, in part, by compositionists, for "the public sphere is always constructed, and it cannot in our society, be unitary" (326). Wells seems to be arguing for a notion of the public sphere as a temporary and unstable meeting of conversants who come together to discuss some topic of mutual interest. She suggests that it is far from the specific, fixed location that is always available, with secure and discernable borders—as we might imagine it. But, she points out, "public space is not available, at least not as we have imagined it" (327). To explain her argument, Wells, like Trimbur before her (and Ward and others, as we shall see, after her) relies heavily on Habermas's critical theory, particularly his treatment of the public sphere, as modified by Oscar Negt and Alexander Kluge.

According to Wells's summary, Habermas posits the public sphere as a discursive domain where private individuals debate social and political issues in an environment free of official or legislative control. The public sphere projects an atmosphere of rational discussion, with no holds barred, no topic off limits. It promises equality of access free of rank and station, with each constituent judged by his (sexist usage appropriate) ability to reason. However, the public sphere, similar to the sites of representative democracy, emerges as a "richly determined practice that produces both knowledge and ignorance, both domination and a diffusion of power" (327). That is, the public sphere is both egalitarian and discordant in the ways discursive interaction occurs. In the public sphere there exists the potential for emancipated participation; in that way, Habermas's conception of it is utopian. But Habermas also recognizes that "the public" implies exclusion and domination as well as openness and reason, since the concept of the private citizen is abstracted from ideas of wealth, property, and privilege. Public discourse, then, is "a complex array of discursive practices, including forms of writing, speech, and media performance, historically situated and contested" (328). Speakers and writers come to the public sphere with both a wealth and a weight of experience; no two constituents can ever be entirely equal. Even the various locations of public discourse, though always shifting and transient, nonetheless have their own histories and possibilities.

Wells suggests that writing projects that are haphazardly assigned as public writing, such as essays on gun control or letters to nonexistent editors, do not "do justice to this history, this set of possibilities" (328). These assignments, no matter how well-written or personally meaningful, are written to no audience whatsoever; they appeal to no particular public sphere. Compositionists, then, must work to create spaces where audiences do exist and where student writing has importance and potential consequences. Creating such spaces is always difficult, and Wells points to the failure of President Clinton's Health Care Address (September 22, 1993) as an example of the difficulties of constructing a public sphere. She suggests that the passion of his speech was "directed, not at health care reform, but at the debate that would make reform possible" (329). Clinton hoped to establish something like a Habermasian public sphere: a space where an issue of public interest could be debated on evidence and reason. Clinton cited the importance of such a debate for the common American, the silent majority. In fact, he mentioned several individuals—a small-businessman and a nurse, among others—as representative citizens. However, Clinton's proposed public sphere was never constructed—suggesting perhaps that the "silent majority" he hoped to appeal to felt that they were unable to free themselves of their silence.

The public sphere, then, is best seen as "contradictory, overdetermined, insoluble, and peremptory—and so it is very close to the experience of the classroom" (332). The public sphere does not adequately represent the experiences of subaltern classes. In fact, it does not even represent all the significant experiences of the ruling classes. It does, though, exist at specific, historical locations. Seen in this light, it is easy to understand why such a site is difficult for students to enter. However, as Wells notes, we are compelled to enter and transform such sites. She writes:

> I have never known a writer, student or teacher, who wanted a smaller
> audience, or a narrower readership; I have never known a writer who felt
> unproblematically at home in the discursive forms of broad political or social
> address. (333)

Given the "intractable fragmentation" of any public sphere, it is likely that the conceptions of the public we offer students beyond the classroom will be provisional and historically situated. Wells, drawing on Negt and Kluge, suggests that we must seek out alternative publics and counter publics that our students might enter. She offers several potential opportunities for public writing, including paired writing assignments with other universities, the collection of oral histories, the establishment of computer networked classes, and community literacy programs.

Unlike Faigley, who has no suggestions for how we might initiate public writing, Wells concludes by suggesting that public writing in a composition course—seen as a relation between readers, texts, and actions—can be organized in (at least) four ways. First, the classroom itself can be seen as a microcosm for public investigation and debate. If the work of the class is seen as reading culture—through critical teaching in cultural studies—this in itself becomes a form of cultural appropriation. The analysis of public texts is a second strategy for teaching public writing. Attention to rhetorical devices and performance inside and outside of texts locates the composition class within the rhetorical tradition. Also, student writing might be generated for real public audiences. Forms of service-learning and discursive activism are powerful kinds of hands-on learning and interaction. Finally, investigations of various discourse communities in academic disciplines, and how they intervene in the public, allows students to recognize the many perspectives that might intersect in the public sphere. Wells offers these pedagogical suggestions in order to help frame a discussion of public writing. While the investigation of the public sphere she offers is far from complete, it has elicited a tremendous response from a number of compositionists. Her article delves into an issue of interest to many compositionists: What *do* we want from public writing? In asking this question, she extends the radical investigation of the political nature of discourse in new directions.

As Wells suggests, the rapid development of computer technology has the potential to open new sites of public discourse. While she mentions the Internet and computer networked classes only briefly, others have explored electronic communication and its possibilities for participatory democratic discourse in more depth. Perhaps the most insightful and lucid investigation of the Internet as a site for meaningful public discourse is Irene Ward's "How Democratic Can We Get? The Internet, the Public Sphere, and Public Discourse." Ward investigates many of the same issues Wells addressed, and she examines some recent claims that the Internet is the new "participatory cyberdemocracy." Ward critiques these claims through the lens of Habermas's account of the public sphere. She makes the point that while the Internet exhibits some organizational features that may facilitate or enhance democratic interaction, we must also remember that "any technology has physical and economic limits, that historical context plays a great role in shaping how technology is used" (365). Ward rightly argues that connecting people through electronic networks does not necessarily lead to a more democratic society, and in fact, the technology itself has the potential to become another tool of dominance and oppression.

To explain her argument, Ward begins with a useful definition of the Habermasian public sphere as a "public institution or place or arena in which private citizens can engage in discussion that is free from any coercive constraints or forms of domination so that by such discussions they can determine matters of general interest or common good" (366). The public sphere brings individuals with different perspectives together for a common goal. Through their interactions, the various constituents in a public sphere have their assumptions challenged; they, in turn, challenge others' assumptions. These constituents, if the public sphere is successful, arrive at some agreement or consensus—what Habermas calls "public opinion." This public opinion, according to Ward, is "more likely to represent true consensus when it is formed in such a public sphere—because it has been subjected to the challenges and questions of a community—than would the aggregate of individual opinions" (367). If the Internet is, or is able to become, a public sphere according to this Habermasian model, it would have to offer an arena for individuals to interact free of constraints. These interactions must have the potential to influence civil society and the state, and the public discourse that is generated in this site must be "legitimized" by the scrutiny and challenge of other citizens and stake holders in the debate.

Does the Internet have the potential to become a true public sphere? Habermas puts forth three institutional criteria that must be met in the establishment of a public sphere. First, it must be a site where little attention is paid to the status of participants. While Habermas fails to acknowledge that this equality has been historically limited to white, male, propertied citizens (more on this critique of Habermas later), his point is that a person, whether he be a merchant or an aristocrat, has an equal right to be heard in the public sphere. Second, the topics debated in the public sphere must be considered of "common concern" to the general public. The conversation could focus on any issue that affects more than one small class in a society. Third, the public sphere must be, at least in principle, inclusive and open to all participants. These participants must be able to think of their conversations as part of a larger public conversation of which they are a small part. Ward suggests that by examining these three criteria in reference to the Internet, we can arrive at a better understanding of the limits and potential of these new sites of "cyberdemocracy."

To what degree does the Internet disregard the status of participants? Since publishing on the Internet is not limited in the same ways as publishing in traditional print media, it seems that cyberspace does disregard the status of the participants. The anonymity of the World Wide Web "can work to focus attention on what is being said over who is saying it" (369). However, access to technology is often limited to the same types of people that had access to public spheres in earlier ages: wealthy white men. While in the past, these constituents were property owners, they have become *technology* owners—people who own or have access to computers.

Is the information found on the Internet of common concern? The Internet might serve as a space where nonspecialists can come together to discuss and interpret cultural artifacts. Due to the relative ease of creating web pages, more and more people are able to create their own cultural products. This seems to promise increased democratization of education: text and materials can be placed on the web with relative ease, for the benefit of institutions and users across the world. However, such projects require budgets of their own, and institutions that produce such materials may not be willing to share their resources with others. It seems reasonable to speculate that wealthy institutions, and the state and local legislatures that fund them, would be better able to compete in this new market and "could end up reestablishing the 'monopoly of interpretation' that the Internet seems to undermine" (372).

Is the Internet generally inclusive? Currently in the United States, there are no institutional or legislative barriers to the Internet for any group or individual. That is, classes of people are not legally or by any set of institutional procedures limited in their use of the World Wide Web. The "cultural lore of the Internet claims that it is and shall remain a domination-free zone for the exchange of ideas and that no amount of encryption software, passwords, government regulation or censorship will be able to obstruct its essentially democratic nature" (373). However, the kinds of access issues I've already described are largely cultural and economic, and they are perhaps more difficult to recognize and eliminate. Those who can afford access—and pay the most for it—will receive the most exposure for their ideas, views, and products. The same social and economic influences that allow for unequal access to education in this country will "operate to make the issue of access a severe limitation to the ultimate democratic potential of the Internet" (375).

Ward rightly points out a number of social, economic, and cultural forces that undermine the possibility of the Internet becoming a democratic sphere. She suggests that some important material circumstances that might lead to the growth of the Internet as a public sphere are not in place. Specifically, the numbers of people who have access to such tools of democracy are not growing as they did in the past. The technology of the Internet does not lend itself to extended interchanges between constituents; rather, it is still "sound-byte technology" suited well to brief, fast exchanges. Computerized telecommunications such as the Internet seem to pose both a potential threat as well as an opportunity for creating public spheres. As writing teachers whose environments are likely to change drastically in the next decades, we will, as Ward notes, have "some exciting and difficult years ahead" (377).

While Ward examines the Internet as a literal site of public writing, other scholars have suggested more figurative uses for the public in composition studies. Joseph Harris offers an interesting perspective on the usefulness of the term "public" for the work we do in the writing classroom. Running through the last thirty or so pages of *A Teaching Subject: Composition Since 1966* is a critique of another metaphor that has been particularly influential in recent discussions of discourse: the *contact zone*. While Mary Louise Pratt's conception of the contact zone as a site where cultures "meet, clash, and grapple with each other" has been a welcome corrective to the relatively unproblematic notion of "community" that dominated social constructionist theories in composition for some time, Harris worries that too many treatments of the contact zone construe it as a "multicultural bazaar" where students are "not so much brought into conflict with opposing views as placed in a kind of harmless connection with a series of exotic others" (119). He proposes the idea of the public as a "more urban and less utopian view of social life [that] might help us rethink the kinds of work that goes on in our classrooms" (108).

Harris suggests that what is most interesting and useful about the term "the public" is that it refers to a space or a location rather than to a particular group (or community) of people. In keeping with Wells, Harris argues that what is most constructive in viewing the classroom as a public space is that it alludes to "a point of contact that needs both to be created and continuously maintained" (109). Harris draws on the work of the social theorist Richard Sennett—another critic of Habermas—who suggests that a public space is one where the members of various communities can meet to negotiate their differences. The metaphor of "public space" implies that it is a site of conflict rather than consensus, a place where constituents come together and bargain out of necessity instead of choice. Harris gives a particularly useful example of how we might imagine such a site:

> The classic example would be a thriving square or market in a cosmopolitan city, It makes little sense to talk of New York, for instance, as a community; it is too sprawling, diverse, heterogeneous. But there is some sense to speaking of it as a kind of public space where the representatives of various boroughs or neighborhoods, the advocates of competing interests or constituencies, can come to argue out their needs or differences. I don't mean here to argue for some idealized version of a public sphere, some free market of viewpoints and ideas. Not all communities or interests are allowed anything near a fair or equal hearing in most public debates, and some are not allowed access to them at all. I am instead thinking of a public space where differences are made visible, and thus where the threat of conflict or even violence is always present. (109)

Harris suggests that thinking of the classroom as a public space rather than a community allows us to imagine it as a site where people negotiate across differences rather than through them. It implies a kind of civility rather than harmonious, serene interaction. Harris imagines a class where students work not to resolve their differences but to highlight them, emphasizing what might be involved in various ways of understanding a text. That is, Harris's notion of the classroom as a public space urges students to see how and why various readers, writers, or speakers might disagree on an issue. Harris calls for a "forum in which issues and concerns that go *beyond* the borders of particular communities or interest groups can be worked through collectively, debated, negotiated" (123). The constituents in such a public space—be they citizens in a city or students in a classroom—need to be willing to come into contact with each other, and they must have some real reason for doing so. They need, as Harris suggests, to feel that they are indeed "citizens of a city and not simply residents of a neighborhood" (123).

SERVICE LEARNING

Recently, a number of scholars in composition and English have foregone questions about what we want from public writing and how we might use the term "public" as a new metaphor for the classroom. These educators have attempted to introduce a form of public writing into their courses through a relatively new approach to teaching: *service learning*. Service learning has moved freely throughout the academy for a number of years, unencumbered by disciplinary identity, moving through education, sociology, psychology, and, most recently, English. Similar to volunteerism, service learning distinguishes itself through its commitment to discourse—particularly its emphasis on reflection. On many campuses, service learning emerged from "student-developed community service programs, while university faculty and staff involvement came later" (Schutz and Gere 129). Service learning combines the sort of democratic action espoused by Freireans, combined with cultural studies approaches that question the nature of the academy to those who surround and support it. Consequently, it asserts that being political in the classroom cannot substitute for the kind of civic participation that is necessary to enact real social and political change in a society. Discussion and reflection of public issues is not enough; action is a necessary component of service learning. As Paul Heilker writes in "Rhetoric Made Real: Civic Discourse and Writing Beyond the Curriculum," writing teachers "need to relocate the *where* of composition instruction outside the academic classroom because the classroom does not and cannot offer students real rhetorical situations in which to understand writing as social action" (71). Service learning approaches to composition attempt to generate situations where writing can be seen as deeply connected to social action and democratic practices.

While many of the articles and books on service learning in English studies have focused on pedagogical, anecdotal tales of how to enact and guide service learning projects, the few that have examined service learning from a theoretical perspective seem to imply a four-step learning cycle for students involved in the project. This model consists of abstract conceptualization, followed by active experimentation, followed by concrete experience, culminating in reflective observation (Adler-Kassner, Crooks, and Waters). Service learning is different from traditional classroom methods in that it has actual, concrete goals that include contact with sites outside of the classroom. Such projects attempt to answer questions about the relevance of postsecondary education through "real world" applications. As such, they work toward easing the identity crisis in English and other disciplines, moving beyond academic discourse and the "ivory tower." As our constituencies—students, taxpayers, legislators—demand greater accountability, service learning projects might increase in size, number, and exposure.

There are a number of benefits touted as part of the service learning model. Students gain academic credit, real-world applications for classroom concepts, real-world work experience for résumés, and a personal investment in the community outside the university. Students are also supposed to develop skills in problem solving and critical thinking. In the process, they develop a more sophisticated analysis of society and their roles in it. The recipients are supposed to benefit through improved literacy or communication skills, new work capabilities, and multicultural awareness. While there are significant obstacles that must be overcome in service learning courses, which some scholars have begun to address, such approaches to public writing seem to be growing exponentially.

According to Bruce Herzberg, service learning helps "put a human face on the students' education" (307). In performing "real and needed services," he says, students discover both "real applications [for] their knowledge in the organizations they serve" *and* "that they can use their knowledge not only to get jobs for themselves but also to help others" (308). However, he notes, students often see those they are helping, such as the homeless, as "people just like themselves." As a result, they often regard social problems as only personal and fail to address systemic explanations for problems in society. Questions about social structures, ideology, and social justice are not automatically raised by service learning projects; in fact, as Herzberg writes, he is "quite sure they are not" (309). If a service learning course is not structured to raise the questions that result in critical analysis of the issues, that course often becomes an exercise in charity rather than education and social change.

Ellen Cushman raises similar questions in her excellent article, "The Rhetorician as an Agent of Social Change." Agreeing with Halloran's desire to reinstitute the rhetorical tradition in composition and English studies, Cushman suggests that we can increase our participation in public discourse by "bridging the university and community through activism" (7). However, she is quick to note that assuming that people will be receptive to activism might very well be a form of "leftist posing disguised as philanthropy" (22). Obviously, service learning projects require negotiation of the sociological distances that need to be crossed. In a related article, Cushman notes the tendency for students to paint themselves as great "liberators of oppressed masses." She writes that one "limitation of service learning courses can be students' perception of themselves as imparting to the poor and undereducated their greater knowledge and skills" (Opinion 332). If the university representatives see themselves as coming to the rescue of community residents, students will enact these same tendencies in their tutoring.

Instructors in the service learning course that Aaron Schutz and Anne Ruggles Gere developed noted that their "students often entered seeing themselves as 'liberal saviors,' and that the structure of tutoring had the potential to enhance the students' vision of this 'savior' role" (133). However, Schutz and Gere are quick to note the benefits of these public projects, particularly when they are rooted in cultural criticism. Echoing Nancy Fraser's criticism of Habermas's public sphere, they suggest that the term "public," when applied to service learning, carries multiple and often conflicting meanings that are always arbitrary and determined by power relations (142). Service learning, like other public writing approaches, requires that we recognize how such practices cannot be disconnected from the issues of power, oppression, and exclusion. Done effectively, service learning could perhaps bring into the curriculum discourses and activities from the world outside of the academy. How service learning proponents negotiate the ideological and sociological obstacles that face such projects will be instrumental in determining the success and endurance of service learning in composition.

Clearly, the idea of the public is currently of great interest to scholars in composition and English studies. What "public writing" might be, however, is uncertain. To some, the public is a useful metaphor for how we might envision the writing classroom. For others, the public is something "out there" that we and our students might attempt to enter through discourse. Some have already attempted to use public writing as a means for bringing about social change. The interest in public writing can be seen as an extension of radical composition, for both examine language use as it enables and inhibits participants in their struggles for public democracy and social justice. As I have noted, discourse specialists have begun to turn to scholarship outside of composition and English studies—most notably the work of cultural theorists such as Jürgen Habermas, Richard Sennett, and Nancy Fraser—to inform their discussions of the public. In composition, scholars including Susan Wells, Irene Ward, Joseph Harris, and Anne Ruggles Gere have recognized the importance of these discussions, and these scholars have incorporated some of this theoretical work into their own examinations of public writing. While many theorists, scholars, and educators have recognized the significance of cultural and social theory to the current conversations in composition and English studies, no scholar has yet put forth a careful and thorough examination of the possibilities of the work of Habermas and others to scholarship on public discourse in English-related fields. The next chapter presents an analysis of cultural theories that inquire into the make-up of public spheres. It also examines the possibilities that educators and intellectuals might have for creating spaces where public discourse can be voiced and heard. By doing so, it provides a fuller understanding of what public writing can or might mean. In the process, it attempts to define what discourse in the public sphere might entail for compositionists in the future.

3

SOCIAL THEORY, DISCOURSE, AND THE PUBLIC SPHERE
New Perspectives on Civic Space

> If we attend to the course of conversation in mixed companies consisting not merely of scholars and subtle reasoners but also of business people and women, we notice that besides storytelling and jesting they have another entertainment, namely, arguing.
>
> —IMMANUEL KANT, *Critique of Practical Reason*

A S I ILLUSTRATED in the second chapter, theories concerning public writing and public spheres are currently of great interest to many scholars in composition in particular and English studies in general. This interest in "the public" as an important concept in writing instruction can be fairly easily traced to more progressive, critical approaches to composition—commonly identified as *radical educationist* perspectives. In the 1990s, radical, critical approaches to composition became more influential and diverse, and one of their most important contributions to composition theory was their problematization of social constructionist theories of composition. These radical approaches were among the first to implicitly critique traditional, teacher-centered methods of writing instruction. Drawing on the work of Paulo Freire and others, the so-called "radicals" in composition have led most composition theorists, researchers, and educators to better understandings of the relationships between power, discourse, and ideology. The interest in public writing has been heavily influenced by radical composition, for both examine language use as it enables and inhibits participants in their struggles for public democracy and social justice. More and more compositionists have recently become interested in moving beyond traditional methods of writing instruction and, consequently, many of the current discussions of writing instruction have begun to theorize pedagogies that move beyond the college or university classroom. That is, many writing instructors today are interested in both theories and practices that allow student writing to have real political and social ramifications, and a few of these educators have made some potentially important and meaningful contributions to discussions of public writing.

What public writing might be, however, is still open to interpretation. To some composition theorists, like Joseph Harris, the term "public" is a useful metaphor for how we might envision the writing classroom in the 1990s and beyond. For others, like S. Michael Halloran and Lester Faigley, public writing necessitates a reorientation to public discourse and a "rhetoric of citizenship" within the writing classroom. Other theorists, including Susan Wells and Irene Ward, have examined composition's desire for efficacious public writing—especially as it is invested in students—and have theorized ways to construct public spheres that students might enter through discourse. Still others have attempted to introduce new forms of public writing into their courses through "service learning."

This new orientation toward public writing and the problems and merits of discourse in the public sphere promises to be an exciting and potentially meaningful direction for the field of composition studies. Like many of the other important movements in writing instruction over the past forty years, the orientation toward public writing will probably develop more sophistication and complexity by turning toward research, theories, and scholarship in other academic disciplines. Just as cognitivist approaches to composition were influenced by inquiries into psychology and social constructionist perspectives were influenced by work in philosophy and the social sciences, a full investigation of public discourse and its place in composition theory will presumably benefit from theories and research in other disciplines. In fact, several of the most influential scholars investigating public discourse have begun to turn to scholarship outside of English studies to inform their discussions of the public— most notably the work of cultural theorists such as Richard Sennett, Jürgen Habermas, Oskar Negt, Alexander Kluge, and Nancy Fraser.

There are many examples of this cross-disciplinary approach to developing a better understanding of public spheres and public discourse. In "Consensus and Difference," John Trimbur draws upon Habermas's theories of communicative action in his critique of collaborative learning. By distinguishing between Habermas's view of consensus, as opposed to the model of consensus advocated by Bruffee and other social constructionists, Trimbur is able to more accurately define consensus as a "critical and normative representation of the conditions necessary for fully realized communication to occur" (612). Susan Wells's more recent "Rogue Cops and Health Care: What Do We Want from Public Writing?" explores Habermas's conceptualization of the public sphere. Much of her argument is rooted in Habermasian cultural theories; through these theories, she is able to more fully account for the public sphere as a discursive domain where private individuals assemble to debate matters of public interest. Wells suggests that it might be helpful to consider how the public and public speech are understood in contemporary theory, and she argues that the "central theorist of the public is Jürgen Habermas" (327). In fact, Wells notes that she bases her argument on "Habermas's treatment of the public sphere, as modified by Oskar Negt and Alexander Kluge" (326). Similarly, Irene Ward's "How Democratic Can We Get? The Internet, the Public Sphere, and Public Discourse" offers an account of the Habermasian public sphere in order to discuss the potential for the Internet to become a public sphere and, consequently, a forum "that private individuals could use to democratically influence the state" (365). Ward notes a number of scholars who have offered modifications of various aspects of Habermas's formulation of the democratic public sphere—most notably, Craig Calhoun, Thomas McCarthy, and Nancy Fraser. In regard to service learning, Aaron Schutz and Anne Ruggles Gere draw upon Hannah Arendt's conceptualization of public spaces. In "Service Learning and English Studies," they posit Arendt's view of the public as a site where individuals are able to "speak, listen, and act together across differences," a postulation that runs counter to Habermas's view of the public, in that Arendt's is a site where differences are recognized rather than disregarded.

Many of these investigations into social and cultural theory have been worthwhile and progressive. They have furthered our understandings of public spheres and public discourse, and they have initiated more discussion on this important topic. They have generated some rudimentary definitions of "the public" and have explored the term's usefulness to composition studies and writing instruction. However, these investigations are far from complete. Nearly all of the discussions regarding the public in composition studies have thus far been merely peripheral; most have been short treatments of at most a few pages, usually situated somewhere within an article or book chapter. These brief investigations have failed to generate a thorough definition of the public sphere and its relationship to work in composition studies. In addition, these inquiries have failed to recognize the public sphere as a historically textured site. That is, most of the current investigations of the public sphere and public discourse in composition studies fail to address the historical, social, and political forces that continually shape and reshape our conceptions of a "public sphere." The public sphere is a complex, sophisticated subject that has been the subject of many books written by cultural theorists, philosophers, and sociologists. While many of the theorists and scholars in composition studies that I mentioned have recognized the importance of theories and discussions emerging from other disciplines, no scholar has yet put forth a careful and thorough examination of the possibilities of the work of Sennett, Habermas, Negt, Kluge, and Fraser to the conversations of the public sphere and public discourse in English studies.

This chapter investigates theoretical conversations concerning the public sphere and considers how these theories are understood in contemporary cultural theory. It begins by providing a historical account of the concept of "the public" as it has been chronicled by Sennett, Habermas, and others. It also explores several of the most important theories concerning the public as it exists today in order to provide a fuller, richer point of departure for compositionists interested in this topic. A careful investigation of the theoretical and philosophical backgrounds of this topic is necessary if compositionists are to inquire into public writing in a competent and thorough manner. By drawing on this large body of scholarship, I hope to outline a more comprehensive theory of the public sphere for composition studies, one that envisions it as a contested, historically textured, multifaceted, and sometimes contradictory site. This provides a point of departure for the full explication of public discourse and its importance to composition theory that follows in chapter 4.

It is important to note at this point that the very use of the term "the public sphere" is subject to scrutiny. The use of the expression "the public sphere" could be misinterpreted to suggest a single site or arena, when the term really represents an abstract concept. Some theorists do envision a singular public sphere arising from the liberal or bourgeois public sphere of the sixteenth and seventeenth centuries and continuing today through various democratic systems. Others suggest that one single conception of the public sphere is inaccurate and that there are, and have been, many public spheres that stand in opposition to the dominant liberal public sphere. In this discussion, I use the term "the public sphere" to stand for the *concept* of the public sphere, not for any actually existing site or sites. That is, while I agree with Negt, Kluge, and Fraser that public discourse has occurred and continues to occur in a variety of overlapping, often contending arenas (more on this later), I see the brunt of the discussions surrounding this topic as dealing with the public sphere as a theoretical abstraction.

Many of these discussions begin with histories of the liberal public sphere and move from there to examine discourse in competing and contesting sites of engagement. While there is a great deal of contention concerning what the concept of the public sphere might actually entail, all of the theorists that I examine here see it as a useful conceptual resource for theorizing the limits of democracy in capitalist societies. Briefly stated, the concept of the public sphere designates a theater in modern democratic societies in which political participation is enacted through discourse. It is the space in which citizens deliberate on matters of common concern and attempt to influence decisions of the state. This arena is conceptually distinct from the state, and, in fact, is in principle *critical* of the state. While I think that all of the theorists that I will discuss would agree on this rudimentary definition of the concept of the public sphere, there seems to be little agreement on where any further discussions or definitions might lead. In the pages that follow, I describe the various discussions of the public sphere to provide the necessary conceptual background for composition theorists interested in this important topic. This background is fundamental to the extended theoretical investigation of public writing found in chapter 4.

ORIGINS OF THE PUBLIC SPHERE

As Jacqueline Jones Royster and Jean C. Williams write in "History in the Spaces Left: African American Presence and Narratives of Composition Studies," history is important, "not just in terms of who writes it and what gets included or excluded, but also because history, by the very nature of its inscription as history, has social, political, and cultural *consequences*" (563). While Royster and Williams make this statement in reference to narratives of the history of composition studies, their point is one that might be applied to the history of the public sphere, if compositionists are to conduct fruitful conversations on the importance of this topic to our work in writing instruction. That is, as a precursor to productive scholarship—and consequently, valuable teaching—on public discourse, it is necessary for compositionists to understand the social, political, and ideological forces that brought about this thing we call the public sphere. The rise of the liberal public sphere is deeply enmeshed in concepts of democracy and liberty, concepts that are at the heart of writing instruction and perhaps even of higher education as a whole. As such, they are plagued with the same historical misreadings and idealizations that have brought us to our current understandings (and misunderstandings) of the public sphere. By understanding the origins and historical variations of the public sphere in Western culture, compositionists might be able to more fully theorize public discourse in the present and future.

The history of public life in Western culture is long and varied, but it does derive from a specific social and cultural milieu. In fact, the first usages of the words "public" and "private" coincide with the fall of monarchy rule, which Richard Sennett identifies as "the *ancien régime*," and the formation of a new capitalist, secular, urban culture (16). Earlier periods in Western culture (and the texts from which we derive our knowledge of them) did not differentiate between these two modes of life. Understanding the history of the words "public" and "private" is fundamental to understanding the emergence of the public sphere as a site where individuals could come together for the purpose of political and social debate.

The first recorded uses of the word "public" in English identify the public with the common good of the majority of individuals in a society. The public as a distinct concept emerged in approximately the late fifteenth century. Central to these early definitions of the public was that it was inherently progressive and often reform-minded.

That is, the term "public" was initially used to mean "in the best interests of the masses." In contrast to "public," the word "private" was initially used to mean "privileged"—"at a high governmental or bureaucratic office or station." It implied a state of seclusion from the common workings of political society, a site where discussion or debate took place among select members of a particular party or coalition. By the end of the seventeenth century, the opposition of the two words "public" and "private" was shaded more like the way we use them today. The two words were no longer restricted in their meanings to purely political engagements, nor did they contain the same connotations of openness and secrecy that they had in their earlier forms. "Public" came to mean open to the scrutiny of anyone, whereas "private" meant a sheltered region of life defined by one's family and close friends. As Richard Sennett notes in *The Fall of Public Man,* there are a number of notable examples of the use of the word "public" in early literary texts. Richard Steele, in an issue of the *Tatler* in 1709, wrote of "These effects . . . upon the publick and private actions of men." Similarly, Samuel Butler wrote in *Sermons* in 1726 that "every man is to be considered in two capacities, the private and the publick." At about the same time, Jonathan Swift also noted the distinction between the two terms, noting that men would go "out in publick" (qtd. in Sennett, 16).

The concept of the public emerged in similar fashion in France during the middle of the seventeenth century. The term *le public* was initially used to describe the common good and the body politic of society during the Renaissance—particularly in Paris. Gradually, this term came to mean a special region of sociability, often having to do with leisure. Sennett notes Erich Auerbach's study of this definition of "the public," which suggests that the first appearances of the term in French were related to the public that was the audience of plays. Not surprisingly, Auerbach discovered that this theatrical audience consisted of an elite group of people. The group of people associated with the term *le public* was a very small group, whose origins were nonaristocratic and mercantile, but "whose manners were directed to obscuring this fact, not only out of shame but in order to facilitate interchanges with the court" (17). That is, *le public* comprised members of the newly formed upper-middle class, members who had not necessarily been born to wealth and affluence but who had very often risen in status and wealth through capitalistic ventures. As such, members of this group hoped to conceal their working-class backgrounds in order to give the appearance of status and promote interactions with the aristocracy.

The sense of who "the public" was, and what it meant to be a member of this group, expanded in the early eighteenth century in both London and Paris. As the number of individuals in the upper-middle class grew, their status and place in society became more secure. For the first time in history, members of a society who were not born to the wealth, status, and power accorded to the aristocracy were able to contribute to political and social decision-making in a society. As Sennett writes:

> Bourgeois people became less concerned to cover up their social origins; there were many more of them; the cities they inhabited were becoming a world in which widely diverse groups in society were coming into contact. By the time the word "public" had taken on its modern meaning, therefore, it meant not only a region of social life located apart from the realm of family and close friends, but also that this public realm of acquaintances and strangers included a relatively wide diversity of people. (17)

"Public" thus came to signify the experiences, relationships, and interactions of individuals outside of the family and close friends. In the public sphere, diverse, complex social groups were brought into contact with one another. The setting for the public sphere was urban, primarily situated in the capital city. As the cities grew in the eighteenth century, both in Europe and in America, they developed networks of sociability independent of direct royal control, places where strangers might regularly meet. The social centers at this time, according to Sennett, consisted of parks, coffeehouses, theaters, pubs, and inns.

It would be incorrect to assume that this expanding public sphere emerged painlessly or justly. Many of the same inequalities of late medieval society were transplanted to this new terrain. The citizens of the eighteenth-century capitals struggled to make sense of the chaotic changes taking place in their world. Sennett suggests that the line drawn between public and private was essentially one on which the "claims of civility—epitomized by cosmopolitan, public behavior—were balanced against the claims of nature—epitomized by the family" (18). These citizens saw these claims in conflict, but they attempted to hold the two in equilibrium. Central to the bourgeoisie was the conception that what separated humans from animals was their ability to interact with strangers in logical, rational exchanges. At the same time, the capacities for love, nurturance, and friendship were felt to be natural, moral, necessary components of a rewarding life.

Sennett suggests that this vibrant public sphere began to break down shortly after the major revolutions of the late eighteenth century, and it has continued to deteriorate since then. He posits that three forces were at work in this change. First, public life in cities came to have a double relationship with industrial capitalism. While public life came to consist more and more of economic, business interactions, the products of these interactions contributed to the degeneration of the public sphere. Mass production of material goods—clothing, for instance—eliminated important physical differences between constituents in the public sphere. Social differences, which were important to success in a rapidly expanding milieu of strangers, became more intractable and mysterious. As a result, individuals became less capable of "reading" the social differences of others in the public sphere.

Sennett notes a second force at work in the decline of public life in the early nineteenth century: it became more confusing and complicated due to the way people interpreted the strange and the unknown. A change in secularism, which Sennett defines as the ways individuals behave and act in society, brought about a new apprehension of the motives and purposes of constituents in the public sphere. Things and people, which were easily assigned a place in nature in the eighteenth century, were no longer seen as quantifiable or understandable. The celebration of objectivity in the eighteenth century gave way to a new way of interpreting public life that posited that the psychological dimensions of negotiation were just as important as the tangible, factual dimensions. The rationalism of the eighteenth century gave way to radical subjectivity. As a result, constituents came to feel that they were unable to distinguish between categories of information, which created a situation that led to mistrust and apprehension in negotiations in the public sphere.

Sennett suggests that a third force was at work in the decline of the public sphere in the nineteenth century: the growth of urban culture in a society that paradoxically preserved the appearance of a vibrant public sphere, while preventing it from more fully transforming. While the other two forces at work continued to erode the public sphere, citizens continued to believe that the experiences of individuals "out in public" were worthwhile and necessary. As a result, no real changes took place in the ways people envisioned public life, and, consequently, no significant alterations were made in the public sphere's basic structure. In the eighteenth century, public experience was connected to the formation of social order; in the nineteenth century, public experience came to be connected to the formation of personality. As Sennett writes, this "painful, unreasonable theme was the conjunction of a surviving belief in the value of public experience" (24). While these three forces do not offer a complete picture of all of the reasons for the decline of the public sphere in the nineteenth century, they do figure as among the most important.

Due to these forces and others, people became less comfortable and secure in their dealings in the public sphere. A new era for public men (women were generally not welcome in the bourgeois public sphere) was ushered in; constituents adopted a more passive approach in their dealings in the public sphere. Spectatorship became the norm. Despite the fact that most individuals were unsure of their ability to express themselves in the public sphere, they continued to believe in its merit. While the ideal of the public sphere continued, it was inhabited by fewer and fewer individuals in the nineteenth and early twentieth centuries. A few people continued to express themselves actively in public. These "active few had by the mid-nineteenth century, become professionals at it; they were skilled performers" (195). The impact of personality on the public identity of the few who were active caused a significant change. These few, most of whom were politicians, began to be judged as believable by whether or not they aroused "the same belief in their personalities which actors did when on stage" (196). The content of political belief and action declined, while people became more and more interested in a politician's personality and charisma.

Sennett suggests that this is the case today. Few people feel capable of active negotiation in the public sphere. Instead, they allow others to stand in for them as representatives. Moreover, they judge the merits of these political representatives through their personalities; what politicians believe has become less and less important in deciding whether or not to support them. The entrance of personality into the public realm in the nineteenth century contributed to the present decline in public life. Political conflicts are interpreted in terms of the play of political personalities; leadership "is interpreted in terms of 'credibility' rather than accomplishment" (219). We may understand that a politician's job is to make rational decisions about public policy, but we are unable to influence him or her, and we are, in fact, uninterested "until we perceive the play of personality in political struggle" (4). A political leader is spoken of as legitimate in terms of what kind of person he or she is, rather than in terms of the actions or programs he or she espouses. According to Sennett, the imbalances in public life over the past century are the result of these various forces and influences. The public sphere has become a shadow of its former self, an eroded version of a once vibrant site of political and social negotiation.

The Habermasian Public Sphere

Perhaps the most important and controversial theorist writing about the public sphere is Jürgen Habermas. The thrust of his work has been to ask when and under what conditions the arguments of mixed companies could become authoritative bases for political action. In *The Structural Transformation of the Public Sphere*, as well as in several other important works, Habermas attempts to theorize a public institution or arena in which private citizens can engage in discussion that is free from any coercive constraints so that through these discussions they can determine matters of general interest or common good. First published in 1962 and reprinted four times since (most recently in English), *Structural Transformation* established the reputation of Habermas as an important figure in social and cultural theory. Originally written as a dissertation for a small circle of scholars, the book soon became a standard work that was to help shape the political consciousness of the new left—most notably the German Frankfurt School—in the 1960s. Habermas draws upon a variety of disciplines in coming to grips with the phenomenon of the public sphere. Like Sennett, Habermas examines the social and historical conditions that gave rise to the public sphere as it exists and functions (or fails to function) in liberal society today. According to Peter Hohendahl, a critic and translator of Habermas, the study "demonstrates that the public sphere constitutes one of the categories central to an understanding of the modern period, i.e. bourgeois society from 1700 to 1974" (45). Habermas focuses on the bourgeois political life of the seventeenth through twentieth centuries in order to determine what conditions led to the growth of a public sphere or spheres, what led to the decline in public discourse, and ultimately, what might be done to promote the renewal of the public sphere in society today.

Habermas posits that the true public sphere was born in Europe in the late seventeenth and early eighteenth centuries. *Structural Transformation* investigates the beginnings of the kind of discourse that claimed to represent general public opinion. Habermas suggests that it is not possible to demonstrate the existence in the European society of the High Middle Ages of a public sphere, in its own right, separate from the private sphere. The concept itself is derived from a concrete historical situation: the rise of capitalism. Before the rise of capitalism, the private sphere encompassed the home, the family and its activities; the public sphere consisted of a relatively small number of individuals who were able to influence judicial, legislative, or governmental decisions. The attribute "public" usually referred to a person endowed with authority. As Habermas writes, "'public' in this narrower sense was synonymous with 'state-related'" (18). Habermas recognizes, of course, that to belong to the public sphere has always meant to wield some share of the ruling power. In the medieval period, as Habermas suggests early in *Structural Transformation,* "*publicare* meant to claim for the lord" (6). This power was, in medieval times, limited to a relatively small number of aristocrats and noblemen. The opening up of markets for foreign trade and the technological developments that facilitated the production of commodities changed the structure of society. These changes brought about a new stratum of people: the *bourgeoisie.*

The typical bourgeois citizen in Europe in the early eighteenth century was unique in that his wealth and status were very often acquired rather than inherited. Of course, Habermas notes that the traditional class structures remained in place, and many of the new bourgeoisie were previously members of the smaller and less influential middle class. However, this new class grew in both number and influence. This stratum of bourgeois people arose to occupy a central position within the emerging public sphere. Habermas notes the rise of this growing class in Germany in the early eighteenth century:

> The old occupational orders of craftsmen and shopkeepers suffered downward social mobility; they lost their importance along with the very towns upon whose citizens' rights their status was based. At the same time, the great merchants outgrew the confining framework of the towns and in the form of companies linked themselves directly with the state. Thus, the "capitalists": the merchants, bankers, entrepreneurs, and manufacturers, (at least where, unlike in Hamburg, the towns could not maintain their independence from the territorial rulers) belonged to that group of the "bourgeois" who, like the new category of scholars, were not really "burghers" in the traditional sense. (23)

This stratum, along with a growing number of doctors, pastors, officers, professors, and scholars, became the leading carriers of the public. It is important to note, as Habermas argues, that this group was from the outset a reading public. Nearly all of them were literate, and as such they were able to more fully and easily communicate with one another and debate in an efficient manner. As a group, many of the bourgeoisie had similar educational backgrounds—a characteristic that helped them form a common ground upon which to communicate. Also, this group began to develop an awareness of the public sphere as "something properly theirs" (24). Earlier manifestations of the middle class were more directly controlled by the state and often assimilated by the cultivated nobility. The commanding status of the new middle class led to tension between the state and civil society. These factors—their growing numbers, their increasing wealth and influence, their literacy and educational backgrounds, and their claim to the public sphere as inherently theirs—contributed to the development of the bourgeois public sphere.

Habermas notes a fairly clear distinction between two separate spheres of bourgeois life, a distinction that contributed to a clearer definition of the public sphere. In opposition to the bourgeois public sphere, the bourgeois private sphere existed "literally in the sphere of the patriarchal conjugal family" (43). As such, it was marked by family, intimacy, and emotion, in contrast to the public values of society, openness, and rationality. The bourgeois private sphere was considered a domestic space inhabited by women and children. Although it was marked by intimacy, it was not considered a hidden space; it was discussed in public as a valuable realm, a necessary component of the "whole" man's life. In this way, its value was confirmed in public. The bourgeois private sphere was often the topic of novels and other literary forms, and these were important in defining the realm of private life. The rise of capitalism strengthened the private sphere. As wealth increased, the bourgeoisie found themselves with more free time and expendable income, both of which they spent on families and close friends.

As capitalism emerged, the numbers of the bourgeoisie grew. These new capitalists (merchants, bankers, manufacturers, and so on) needed to gain the cooperation of the state if capitalism was to continue its growth. The new bourgeois society aimed to influence the state and limit its control over judicial, legislative, and governmental decisions. This stratum was affected by state mercantile and trade policies more than any other. They became more aware of their dependence upon measures taken by the state administration, whose intent was to control commercial-entrepreneurial activity and regulate trade in order to maintain state control over wealth and power. The traditional powers of the state (the aristocracy and the church), who had for so long controlled the legislation dealing with trade and manufacturing, were relatively unconcerned with the developing market economy. The bourgeoisie sought to transform the state to an "authority restricted to a limited number of functions and supervised by the public" (Held 261). As a result, these two forces were initially at odds with each other. The bourgeoisie hoped to diminish the power and influence of the state in matters relating to trade and commerce. According to Habermas,

> mercantilism did not at all, as widespread prejudice would have it, favor state enterprise; rather, its commercial policy, albeit in a bureaucratic fashion, promoted the establishment and dissolution of private businesses run in a capitalist manner. The relationship between the authorities and the subjects thereby assumed the peculiar ambivalence of public regulation and private initiative. In this way the zone in which public authority, by way of continuous administrative acts, maintained contact with private people, was rendered problematic. (24)

Since these two forces were at odds, the zone of contact between them became critical to the bourgeoisie. In order to facilitate their interactions with the state and also continue their growth and new prominence, the bourgeoisie began to develop a public sphere. Habermas conceives of the bourgeois public sphere as "a forum in which private people, come together to form a public, readied themselves to compel public authority to legitimize itself before public opinion" (25–26). Habermas, as we can see, is somewhat equivocal on the subject of power. As I've noted, he recognizes that belonging to the public sphere in earlier ages—he mentions the medieval period specifically—meant to command a portion of the ruling power in a society. However, his later definition stops short of recognizing the power manifested in the public sphere. He fails to address any immediate implementation of the opinions produced by the public sphere's free and spirited conversation. He notes that the bourgeois public "*readied* themselves to *compel* public authority" (27). This definition delineates the public sphere not as a site for the compulsion itself, but only for readying oneself to compel. Even that compulsion, had it been realized, was only a compulsion for the authorities to engage in further dialogue. Habermas fails to recognize the power that those who occupied the bourgeois public sphere controlled and he neglects to account for the cultural, ideological, and historical circumstances that put them there in the first place. As Bruce Robbins asks in his introduction to *The Phantom Public Sphere:*

> How can Habermas explain even this anticipatory, as yet unused ability to exert compulsion upon the government without examining the power that those who occupy the public sphere draw from historically specifiable sources, sources other than wit—from their cultural capital, from their gender and race, from the Industrial Revolution, and so on? For Habermas, as many critics have pointed out, the golden age of the public sphere is the long moment of bourgeois revolution. . . . Yet this is a power that, while riding piggyback on a rising class, pretends not to be or even touch power. (xx–xxi)

This failure to fully address the issue of power and ideology in the bourgeois public sphere is one of the primary criticisms of Habermas's work. As I shall show later in this chapter, a number of critics have put forth some compelling and important commentaries on this aspect of Habermas's conception of the bourgeois public sphere.

Despite Habermas's equivocation on the nature of power in the public sphere, the eighteenth century bourgeoisie obviously believed that the public sphere was an inherently powerful yet impartial domain. According to Habermas, the bourgeoisie claimed that "the public sphere regulated from above against the public authorities themselves, to engage them in a debate over the general rules governing relations in the basically privatized but publicly relevant sphere of commodity exchange and social labor" (*Structural Transformation* 27). That is, the bourgeoisie asserted that the public sphere was a neutral site where the actions of the state were brought under scrutiny. In Great Britain and France in the early eighteenth century, this public sphere began to take shape in coffeehouses, salons, societies, newspapers, and periodicals of all kinds. Obviously, these various venues for public debate differed in the size and composition of their publics, the style of their proceedings, the climate of their debates, and their topical orientations. However, they all organized discussion among private people that tended to be ongoing. That is, the discussions and interactions among individuals in the bourgeois public sphere often occurred over a series of related occasions.

Institutional Criteria of the Bourgeois Public Sphere

Habermas suggests that since the discussions in these various public spheres were ongoing, they had a number of institutional criteria in common. First, he writes, "they preserved a kind of social intercourse that, far from presupposing the equality of status, disregarded status altogether" (36). Habermas supposes that the bourgeois public sphere was a site of mutual interaction, an arena where constituents overlooked the backgrounds, credentials, and lineages of other citizens. In opposition to earlier groups that had engaged in political and social discourse—groups that had recognized status as the primary basis for the right to speak and be heard—a central tenet of the bourgeois public sphere was that it ignored status. Habermas argues that this "tendency replaced the celebration of rank with a tact befitting equals" (36). Not only were power and prestige "held in suspense," as Habermas writes, "economic dependencies also in principle had no influence" (36). That is, this first criterion of the bourgeois public sphere was that it assumed a social leveling of all participants.

While Habermas glosses over the degree to which status, rank, class, race, and gender were still very much present in the bourgeois public sphere—a significant element of contention among his various critics—he does acknowledge that it was limited to a certain segment of the population. Habermas recognizes that "private gentlemen" made up the public; the public sphere was largely restricted to white males who were propertied. However, social status no longer *guaranteed* that one's voice would be heard. For perhaps the first time in history, it was less likely that an aristocrat or religious leader would be deferred to in a public discussion. As Irene Ward writes, "merchant, aristocrat, and bishop alike had to prove their worth to the gathering by the quality of their public discourse" (368). Habermas also acknowledges that the parity that the bourgeois public aspired to was not "actually realized in earnest in the coffee houses, the salons, and the societies" (*Structural Transformation* 36). The equality they asserted was never actually achieved. Nevertheless, as an idea it had become institutionalized and was stated as an objective claim. While parity was not realized, the claimed desire for it was at least consequential. The bourgeois public sphere posited the value of open participation even though it could not fulfill it.

The second institutional criterion of the bourgeois public sphere was that new subjects must have been considered of "common concern" to the general public. Discussion within this public sphere was grounded on the idea that areas that had previously been off-limits were now problematized and questioned. At first, this took the form of bourgeois discussions of the merits of art, music, and literature—subjects that had previously been confined to aristocrats and noblemen. The commodification of cultural products made them more generally available to the public, taking them out of the control of the church and state and making them accessible to anyone who could purchase them. In the process, they lost their air of sacredness and exclusivity. Habermas writes:

> To the degree, however, to which philosophical and literary works and works of art in general were produced for the market and distributed through it, these cultural products became similar to that type of information: as commodities they became in principle generally accessible. They no longer remained components of the Church's and court's publicity of representation; that is precisely what was meant by the loss of their aura of extraordinariness and by the profaning of their once sacramental character. The private people for whom the cultural product became available as a commodity profaned it inasmuch as they had to determine its meaning on their own (by way of rational communication with one another), verbalize it, and thus state explicitly what precisely in its implicitness for so long could assert its authority. (36–37)

Habermas suggests that in the salons especially, individuals from mixed positions gathered to discuss and critique art, literature, plays, music, and opera. Over time, the influence of the market economy expanded these conversations to encompass philosophy, economics, and politics as well. Cultural products came to be produced for and consumed by the growing middle class. The church and state were no longer the primary consumers and regulators of art and literature through patronage. With the loss of church and state patronage of the arts came the loss of their "monopoly of interpretation" of those cultural artifacts. As Ward writes, "those who were interested could and did interpret works of art, literature, philosophy, and even economic and political texts through conversations at the societies, salons, and coffeehouses, and in the popular press" (371–72). The power to decide what any particular cultural artifact might mean was no longer decided by a select few, but was open to interpretation by a much broader segment of society.

Habermas notes a third criterion of the bourgeois public sphere: accessibility. These public forums were "in principle" inclusive; everyone had to be *allowed* to participate. While these assemblies certainly did not represent all segments of society in seventeenth- and eighteenth-century Europe, they were considered to be inclusive by the participants because they came to think of their conversations as small segments of a larger, more extensive public conversation of which they were a small part. That is, the constituents who gathered in these public forums considered themselves to be part of a larger public. The issues that were discussed became "general" not merely in their subject matter, but also in their accessibility. Habermas argues that

however exclusive the public might be in any given instance, it could never
close itself off entirely and become consolidated as a clique; for it always
understood and found itself immersed within a more inclusive public of all
private people, persons who—insofar as they were propertied and educated—
as readers, listeners, and spectators could avail themselves via the market of
the objects that were subject to discussion. (37)

Habermas, to his credit, recognizes that the bourgeois public sphere actually comprised
a small segment of the general population. Although literacy rates had risen substantially, much of the population, especially in rural areas, was still illiterate and unable
to participate in the public sphere. More than half of the population in Great Britain
lived on the margins of subsistence and were too involved with securing necessities
to be concerned with public discourse. The bourgeois public sphere, as Habermas
describes it, was male, educated, and propertied. In fact, in France, the conflation of
the terms *bourgeois* and *homme,* of property owner and human being, provided the
bourgeois public sphere with a unity—even though it was a fictive one. A document
like the Declaration of Independence, for example, provided unity through its assertion that "all men are created equal," while at the same time it excluded all but land-
owning, white male citizens. Nevertheless, the idea of unfettered access was central
to the bourgeois public sphere, and as such it represents an opening—one that could
potentially become more open. As Habermas writes, the "public sphere of civil society stood or fell with the principle of universal access" (85)

As I have noted, Habermas argues that it was in the bourgeois public sphere of
coffeehouses, salons, societies, newspapers, and periodicals of all kinds that this new
social order took shape. These were the forums for public debate by private persons,
and, according to Habermas, the bourgeois public sphere reached the height of its
power and influence in the eighteenth century. He also notes that literacy was one of
the most important aspects of the bourgeois public sphere. The stabilization of a "reading culture" was central to social and political power. The institutions of this reading
public prepared the groundwork for a political public sphere. The influx of rational-
critical arguments in the popular press allowed them to evolve into "instrument[s] with
whose aid political decisions could be brought before the new forum of the public"
(58). Newspapers and gazettes grew dramatically in terms of their circulation and
influence, and most of them were designed to influence politics and motivate social
change. They transformed from being reporters of factual information to leaders of
public opinion. Book clubs brought the ideas of liberal writers like Swift, Pope, and
Gay to an increasingly vocal and influential public. The public opinion that was formed

in these forums was thought by the participants to represent the general interests of the people. This public sphere thrived for some time, both in Europe and in America in the eighteenth century.

Gradually though, as Habermas suggests, the bourgeois public sphere eroded. This erosion can be "clearly documented with regard to the transformation of the public sphere's preeminent institution, the press" (181). As Habermas suggests, newspapers had transformed from institutions for the publishing of news to instruments in the "arsenal of party politics" (182). Over time, as more and more political journals emerged and censorship of them loosened, the press was released from its obligation to take sides ideologically, and they reverted to more factual, depoliticized interpretations of newsworthy information. In the process, newspapers began to concentrate more exclusively on profit. Habermas suggests that in "Great Britain, France, and the United States at about the same time (the 1830s) the way was paved for this sort of transition from a press that took ideological sides to one that was primarily a business" (184)

As newspapers and other forums for public debate became more and more occupied with their own commercial success and less with political and social change, the bourgeois public sphere disappeared. Finally, with the emergence of welfare-state mass democracy, society and the state became mutually intertwined; "publicness" in the sense of critical scrutiny gave way to public relations, mass-mediated staged displays and the manufacture and manipulation of public opinion. Nevertheless, Habermas suggests that the kind of public discourse that formed in seventeenth- and eighteenth-century Europe and America could provide a model, or at least a starting point, for how more inclusive forms of the public sphere might be formed in the present and future.

Habermas's contribution to the analysis of the bourgeois public sphere rests on a number of significant points. Primarily, Habermas attempts to reconstruct the public sphere as a fundamentally *historical* category. In other words, he suggests that the concept of the public sphere can never be fully understood unless it is examined in relation to the historical, political, ideological, and contextual factors that brought about its emergence, contributed to its growth and prominence, and led to its decline. While this analysis implies that the bourgeois public sphere was the only actually existing public sphere in history, Habermas does seem to think that a similar sphere could emerge in the future. He suggests that the bourgeois public sphere is an essentially historical concept, linked to the formation of bourgeois society under liberal capitalism. Also, he delineates the public sphere as a primary category of human existence. He posits that the "public" can be seen as a fourth term of human social life, distinct from the state, the marketplace, and the intimate sphere of the family. His work is certainly indispensable to any discussion of the public sphere.

Negt and Kluge's Critique of the Habermasian Public Sphere

When Habermas published *The Structural Transformation of the Public Sphere* in 1962, it was recognized as a groundbreaking study of the public sphere, while at the same time it was critiqued as being anachronistic, overly optimistic, and conservative. As it was originally published only in German, nearly all of the subsequent deliberations concerning it were published in European books and journals. Nearly thirty years later in 1989, Thomas Burger translated the work into English. Almost immediately, British and American intellectuals recognized the importance of *Structural Transformation,* and the work soon became a significant topic of discussion among sociologists, historians, cultural theorists, and philosophers. Although many critiques of the work have been written and published in English, one of the first thorough analyses of Habermas's work was also originally published in German: Oskar Negt and Alexander Kluge's *Public Sphere and Experience: Toward an Analysis of the Bourgeois and Proletarian Public Sphere.* Translated into English in 1993, just four years after the translation of *Structural Transformation,* the work has been recognized as an important contribution to the discussions of the public sphere.

Negt and Kluge carry on some of the most significant aspects of Habermas's project while at the same time critiquing a number of the foundations upon which Habermas's interpretation of the public sphere is based. They hold out the belief that a public sphere did—and can—exist in a capitalist society. For example, in an interview in the journal *October,* Alexander Kluge states: "Our notion of *Öffentlichkeit,* or publicness, is not really opposed to Habermas's. It is a response as part of a process of discussion" (42). They also agree with Habermas's interpretation of the historicity of the public sphere. Like Habermas, they agree that, in order to fully understand what the bourgeois public sphere consists of, it is necessary to look at the political, cultural, and ideological forces that helped shape it. This interpretation is often quite difficult, they suggest, as the meaning of the term "public" transformed and mutated in relation to its historical contexts. They write:

> It is difficult to determine the use-value of the public sphere because it is a historical concept of extraordinary fluidity. The use of the terms "public" and "public sphere" reveals a diversity of competing meanings. These derive from different historical phases and, when applied simultaneously to the conditions of an industrially advanced society and the welfare state, amount to an opaque combination. (1)

Despite the difficulty of accurately interpreting and describing the public sphere's various historical manifestations, Negt and Kluge agree with Habermas that the public sphere is a central facet of human social life. They write that the public sphere is "a genuine articulation of a fundamental social need. It is the only form of expression that links the members of society to one another by integrating their developing social characteristics" (2).

Despite the fact that Negt and Kluge are in accord with Habermas on some of the most rudimentary definitions of the public sphere, most of their work critiques Habermas's analysis of the bourgeois public sphere. One of their most significant critiques of Habermas is that he idealizes the bourgeois public sphere. Specifically, they question the lack of attention to issues of difference and ideology in his conception of the public sphere. They suggest that Habermas posits an Enlightenment ideal of equality and impartiality in the public sphere. However, this utopian vision of the bourgeois public sphere is quite different from its "historical realization." The contradictions, shortcomings, and imperfections of the bourgeois public sphere, Negt and Kluge argue, do not just emerge with the disintegration of the public sphere in the seventeenth and eighteenth centuries; rather, they are inherent in the very constitution of that public sphere. The bourgeois public sphere was founded on the principles of generality, inclusiveness, and consensus. These ideals are in opposition to particularity, exclusivity, and individuality. However, this principle of generality—the bracketing of social status and special interest—is no more democratic than the capitalist market it presumes to set aside. While the founders and leaders of the bourgeois public sphere claimed inclusiveness as a primary characteristic, their public sphere was also based upon the desire to increase capitalism and facilitate commodity production. In this way, the bourgeois public sphere "excludes from politics and the public sphere all those sections of the population that do not participate in bourgeois politics because they cannot afford to" (10). That is, the bourgeois public sphere was (and still is) constructed by and for those in control of material goods and production. As Negt and Kluge write, "the construction of the public sphere derives its entire substance from the existence of owners of property" (10).

In fact, Negt and Kluge argue that the bourgeois property owners were never really interested in developing a truly public sphere that was open to all segments of society. They intended only to develop a network of relations between others like them and thereby gain power and influence in their relations with the state. Negt and Kluge argue that

> the bourgeois property owners . . . were not interested in the formation of
> public experience. Their knowledge of the market is private. In relation to the
> state and the public sphere, their prime interest is in the possible countereffects

of this public sphere on their private interests. What was strictly an end in itself
. . . was merely a means for the real bourgeois public society. (10)

Negt and Kluge suggest that the public sphere was used as a tool by the bourgeoisie,
a method for increasing their ability to create markets for their goods, facilitate trade,
and generate profit for themselves and their peers. They used the ideals of consensus, equality, openness, and the like to create favorable situations. They did not, according to Negt and Kluge, consider the public sphere to be a primary aspect of their
lives. Instead, they used it to improve their own private circumstances. They write:

> The public sphere widened the perspective on appropriation for whole groups
> of capitalists: they attempt to acquire contracts to supply the army, to float
> public loans; they want to become involved in public works, to appropriate
> state authority so as to strengthen and protect property interests, to secure
> advantageous positions in world trade by means of gunboat diplomacy and
> tariffs, to win state protection for colonial exploitation. For the ruling class, this
> framework of the public sphere was in any case not the real horizon of their
> social experience and formation of opinion, but merely a subsidiary aspect.
> "Having experience" within this public sphere meant to have dominant
> knowledge—a specialized knowledge of how to exploit this public sphere
> properly. This knowledge includes the capacity to cloak the immediate
> fractionalized interests of capital in the form of an imagined sovereignty, a
> feigned collective will. (11)

The bourgeois public sphere was, then, a subterfuge through which private individuals of rank and status increased their domination of others and monopolized the means
and ends of capitalism. As Dana Polan writes in "The Public's Fear," Negt and Kluge
"work hard to show that the bourgeois public sphere was much more run through by
the interests of capitalist exchange than Habermas wants to admit" (37).

   In contrast to Habermas, Negt and Kluge insist on the need to understand postbourgeois public formations in terms other than those of disintegration and decline.
In fact, they insist that no singular form of the public sphere every truly existed, nor
will it in the future. In her Foreword to Negt and Kluge's book, Miriam Hansen suggests that "it is impossible to define or describe Öffentlichkeit in the singular, as if it had
any homogeneous substance" (xxix). Rather, it is best understood as an accumulation
of phenomena at a variety of locations. Negt and Kluge argue for a vision of public
life that implies a field of discursive connections rather than an individual, common
arena. They suggest—as do a number of critics of Habermas—that he makes the mis-

take of imagining that there must be one public sphere. Instead, Negt and Kluge argue for a notion of multiple, overlapping, and often contending public spheres. This notion of alternative or counterpublics is one of their most compelling lines of thought—one that, as I shall show, has been taken up by other cultural theorists such as Nancy Fraser. Negt and Kluge understand the public sphere "as an aggregation of phenomena that have completely diverse characteristics and origins." They go on to state that "the public sphere has no homogeneous substance whatsoever" (13). In their attempt to make sense of this "aggregation of phenomena," they distinguish three different types of public life. However, they make the point that these cannot be viewed in isolation from one another; these modes of social experience must be seen as "mutually imbricated," overlapping, cohabitational, and often contradictory. While they do recognize the "classical" bourgeois model of the public sphere, they also acknowledge "public spheres of production" and the "proletarian public sphere."

Public spheres of production, according to Negt and Kluge, differ from the classical bourgeois public sphere in that their relationship to capitalism and the production of goods and services is much more apparent. While the classical model of the public sphere asserts its openness, impartiality, and objectivity in relation to capitalism, public spheres of production are created in the contexts of capitalism. They no longer pretend to be a separate sphere above the marketplace but are an "immediate expression" of the process of production. Negt and Kluge argue that "the classical public sphere is originally rooted in the bourgeois context of living, yet separates itself from the latter and the production process. By contrast, the new public spheres of production are a *direct expression of the sphere of production*" (13). These spheres of production occur at a variety of locations, ranging from factory communities and corporate public relations, through various spaces of commerce and consumption, to privately owned forms of mass media. Their relationships with the classical public sphere are often reciprocal; they often graft themselves onto the remnants of a bourgeois public sphere for legitimacy and force. Negt and Kluge suggest that branches of the mass media are particularly good examples of this. They cite televised news broadcasts of judicial and legislative debates as just one example of this reciprocal relationship. The former (the news broadcasts) gain legitimacy and respectability while the latter (the debates) gain a more comprehensive horizon. These alliances usually work to reproduce dominant ideology, and, above all, "to simulate the fictive coherence and transparency of a public sphere that is not one" (Hansen xxx).

As a "counterconcept" to both bourgeois and industrial-commercial variants of "publicness," Negt and Kluge offer the notion of a proletarian public sphere. They suggest that the concept of a proletarian public sphere is somewhat ambiguous, although it "does refer to a strategic position that is substantively meshed with the history of the emancipation of the working class" (xliv). They argue for a view of the proletarian public sphere as a "crystalizing point"; a public sphere that reflects the interests and experiences of the overwhelming majority of the population. They view this proletarian public sphere as a counterpublic that embodies the "experiential interests" of the working class, experiences that have and continue to run in opposition to the bourgeois public sphere. This counterpublic develops in the midst of historical fissures—crises, war, revolution—and is comprised of "concrete constellations of social forces" (xliii). Since it has no existence as a ruling public sphere, it has to be constructed from these rifts. The proletarian public sphere often consists of marginal cases and isolated initiatives that confront dominant public spheres. Often, these counterpublic spheres appropriate the forms, discourses, settings, and structural methods of the controlling spheres. Negt and Kluge write:

> It is essential that the proletarian counterpublic sphere confronts these public spheres, which are permeated by the interests of capital, and does not merely see itself as the antithesis of the classical public sphere. . . . At stake is a practical, political experience of the working class: the working class must know how to deal with the bourgeois public sphere and must know what threats the latter poses, without allowing its own experiences to be defined by the latter's narrow horizons. The bourgeois public sphere is of no use as a medium for the crystallization of the particular experience of the working class—it is not even the real enemy. Since it came into being, the labor movement's motive has been to express politically proletarian interests in its own forms of public sphere. At the same time, the goal has been to contest the ruling class' enlistment of the state. (xlvii)

The proletarian public sphere, then, recognizes the bourgeois processes of exclusion and suppression from the position of the marginalized working classes. As Miriam Hansen writes, without "using the Gramscian term, they describe mechanisms of exclusion and silencing as hegemonic principles and, conversely, formulate the contestation of those principles from the position of the subaltern" (xxx). Whereas Habermas suggested that the bourgeois public sphere was the primary sector of human life that challenged or inflected the course of state policy, Negt and Kluge deemphasize the importance of the bourgeois public sphere and extend the notion of politics to all social sites of production and interaction. They question Habermas's assumption that human experience is organized "from above," and they suggest that the experiencing subjects themselves contribute to organizing experience "from below." The proletarian public sphere, while always influenced by the bourgeois public sphere, the public sphere of production, and other systems of domination, is capable of some degree of self-determination.

The proletarian public sphere, then, is "ultimately a radical form of democracy [that] involves not just the empowerment of constituencies hitherto excluded from the space of public opinion, but also a different principle of organization, a different concept of public life" (Hansen xxxi). Negt and Kluge note several examples of the proletarian public sphere that have already emerged in the past, including the Italian Maximalist Party in the 1920s and certain moments in the October Revolution. Ironically though, the concept of the proletarian public sphere could be discursively constructed as a result of its negation by the dominant public sphere. That is, hegemonic efforts to suppress, fragment, delegitimize, or assimilate alternative or counterpublics by the dominant public reaffirms their potential for action. By negating them through discourse, the dominant public sphere suggests that alternative, divergent publics could potentially exist.

The discursive construction of these counterpublics is essential to their development and success. In fact, it could be argued that the notion of the proletarian public sphere is essentially an effort to produce a critical or analytic discursive space. Negt and Kluge argue for the creation of new discursive forms in order to legitimize emerging counterpublics. They argue that these discursive forms must be the original products of the masses and cannot be created in dominant or academic spheres. While the bourgeois public sphere rests upon a specific, often specialized discursive form, Negt and Kluge suggest that the proletarian public sphere must use language that has been constructed from the direct experiences of the masses. They argue for "diction close to the people" in order to unite disparate factions of the working class. Written and spoken language might be enriched by words that do not derive from educated language but are created through the histories and backgrounds of the masses. As an example, they write:

There is a similar phenomenon in the linguistic practice of East Germany— under quite different social circumstances. Expressions are used that incorporate elements of the production process but do not correspond to standard language. There are, for instance, countless expressions for the correct way to tighten metal parts and screws. The use of these in politics transfers collective social experience to the solving of political problems. I can say: "Despite long reflection I have not found the tactical political solution to this problem," but I can also express myself as follows: "I've been up and about since five this morning thinking about this problem. I just can't get a lead on it." A pedant would regard this as bad style. Such a way of expressing oneself would be alien to the educated elite of the nineteenth century. Yet in reality it represents an enrichment of language. Such an enrichment is a direct function of the politicization of society. This presupposes a politicization of the forms of expression, which is supplied neither by educated language nor by the colloquial language spontaneously developing alongside standard language, nor by the professional language of science or technical specialists. (273)

They argue, then, that original language constructions that arise from the experiences of subjugated or oppressed classes of people are not unseemly or incorrect, as a member of the dominant class might argue. Such language serves a political function in that it gives power of expression to the subaltern. While Negt and Kluge's theories that posit the value of discourse emerging from the experiences of disenfranchised groups were published over twenty-five years ago, they are quite similar to the postcolonial studies of subaltern discourses by scholars such as Homi K. Bhabha, Gayatri Spivak, and Edward Said—studies that have become prominent in some of the most recent conversations in composition theory. Negt and Kluge's *Public Sphere and Experience* offers a more critical interpretation of the public sphere, one that posits the construction of counterpublics and the possibilities of experiential linguistic practices within them. As Fredric Jameson writes in "On Negt and Kluge,"

> The originality of Negt and Kluge, therefore, lies in the way in which the hitherto critical and analytic force of what is now widely known as "discourse analysis" (as in Foucault's descriptions of the restrictions and exclusions at work in a range of so-called discursive formations) is now augmented, not to say completed, by the utopian effort to produce discursive spaces of a new type. (49)

Nancy Fraser's "Rethinking" of the Public Sphere

Negt and Kluge's critique of the public sphere is perhaps most useful in that it questions the universalizing ideal of a single public and considers public spheres that might affirm the lived experiences of working, proletariat, and subaltern classes. Their work moves away from theories of the public sphere that claim to overlook or "bracket" the roles of power, ideology, and difference and toward a conception of public spheres that envisions them as a multiplicity of distinct and overlapping discourses and sites of negotiation. One of the most engaging analyses of the public sphere published during the past decade is Nancy Fraser's "Rethinking the Public Sphere: A Contribution to the Critique of Actually Existing Democracy." Her article, first published in Craig

Calhoun's *Habermas and the Public Sphere* and later reprinted in Bruce Robbins's *The Phantom Public Sphere,* suggests that Habermas's work is most useful in that it distinguishes between the apparatuses of the state on the one hand and public arenas of citizen discourse and association on the other. She notes that this conflation is "a confusion one encounters at times in contemporary feminisms" (110).

While Fraser argues that the general idea of the public sphere—and its distinction from the realm of the state—is indispensable to critical theory, she suggests that the specific form in which Habermas has elaborated this idea is not wholly satisfactory. She contends that "his analysis of the public sphere needs to undergo some critical interrogation and reconstruction if it is to yield a category capable of theorizing the limits of actual existing democracy" (111). Fraser acknowledges Habermas's assertion that some new form of the public sphere is required to salvage the arena's critical function and to institutionalize democracy. However, she questions the fact that he stops short of developing a new model of the public sphere and fails to adequately problematize some dubious assumptions that underlie the bourgeois model. As a result, she suggests, we are "left at the end of *Structural Transformation* without a conception of the public sphere that is sufficiently distinct from the bourgeois conception to serve the needs of critical theory today" (112).

Fraser begins by suggesting that Habermas's account idealizes the bourgeois public sphere. Just as radical compositionists argued that social constructionist theories of discourse do not account for the influences of power and ideology, Fraser suggests that Habermas's notion of the liberal public sphere does not recognize the degree to which an individual's race, class, and gender affect their ability to speak in public settings. She notes a number of scholars, including Joan Landes, Mary Ryan, and Geoff Eley, who suggest that "despite the rhetoric of publicity and accessibility, the official public sphere rested on, indeed was importantly constituted by, a number of significant exclusions" (113). Fraser agrees with these critics, arguing that exclusionary practices were fundamental to nearly all liberal public spheres in Europe in the seventeenth and eighteenth centuries. Gender exclusions, in particular, were linked to other exclusions rooted in the processes of class formation. The "public spheres" that emerged at this time were anything but accessible to everyone, and they became the "power base of a stratum of bourgeois men who were coming to see themselves as a 'universal class' and preparing to assert their fitness to govern" (114). Ironically, she notes, the very discourse that touted accessibility, rationality, and the suspension of status functioned as a "marker of distinction" in that it was used nearly exclusively by propertied white males.

Not only does Habermas idealize the bourgeois public sphere, he also fails to examine other nonliberal, nonbourgeois, competing public spheres. Fraser argues that

women of various classes and ethnicities constructed "access routes" to public political life, despite their exclusion from the "official" public sphere. This involved the organization of voluntary associations, street protests, moral-reform societies, and suf-
frage movements. Thus, the view that women had no part in the public sphere is
ideologically interested; it "rests on a class- and gender-based notion of publicity, one
that accepts at face value the bourgeois public's claim to be *the* public" (116). Fraser
rightly notes that a host of competing counterpublics arose virtually in tandem with the
bourgeois public sphere. These counterpublics contested the exclusionary practices
of the bourgeois public from the very beginning, through alternative styles of political behavior and different forms of public discourse. This revisionist view suggests a
radically different conception of the public sphere than the one Habermas puts forth.
Fraser writes that we can no longer "assume that the bourgeois conception of the
public sphere was simply an unrealized utopian ideal; it was also a masculinist ideological notion that functioned to legitimate an emergent form of class rule" (116). Thus,
the emergence of the bourgeois public sphere marks a shift from a more obtrusive,
repressive mode of domination to a hegemonic one. That is, the dominant power in
European society shifted from a mode based upon overt authority and the acquies-
cence to superior force to one based upon imagined consent and subtle manipulation.

Rather than dispensing with the concept of the public sphere, Fraser proposes a
more nuanced interpretation of the bourgeois public sphere. Her alternative interro-
gates four basic aspects of the Habermasian bourgeois public sphere. She argues that
"the revisionist historiography neither undermines nor vindicates *the* concept of the
public sphere *simpliciter,* but that it calls into question four assumptions that are central to the *bourgeois, masculinist* conception of the public sphere, at least as Habermas
describes it" (117).

First, Fraser questions the assumption that it is possible for interlocutors in a public sphere to actually bracket status differentials and to deliberate as if they were social equals. The assumption that Habermas seems to make is that societal equality is
not a necessary precondition for political democracy. Habermas's interpretation of the
bourgeois public sphere, as I have already noted, was one that posits it to have been
an arena where individuals would set aside "such characteristics as differences in birth
and fortune and speak to one another as if they were social and economic peers" (118).
Were the social differences among interlocutors in the bourgeois public sphere effectively bracketed? Fraser suggests that they were not:

> Rather, discursive interaction within the bourgeois public sphere was governed
> by protocols of style and decorum that were themselves correlates and
> markers of status inequality. These functioned informally to marginalize

women and members of the plebeian classes and to prevent them from participating as peers. (119)

Much like Evelyn Ashton-Jones's critique of collaboration, conversation, and consensus in social constructionist approaches to composition, Fraser cites recent feminist research that has documented conversational dynamics in mixed-sex deliberations. These, as I have noted in the previous chapter, include the fact that men interrupt women more often, tend to speak more often than women, take longer turns speaking, and ignore women's responses and questions. Fraser notes that many of these feminist insights into the ways in which deliberation can serve as a mask for domination extend beyond gender to other kinds of unequal relations, like those based on class or ethnicity.

This critique questions one of the very bases of Habermas's interpretation of the bourgeois public sphere: that it provided participatory parity. The bracketing of differences in deliberation does not necessarily provide equal access; on the contrary, "such bracketing usually works to the advantage of dominant groups in society and to the disadvantage of subordinates" (120). In fact, Fraser argues that it would be more appropriate to *unbracket* inequalities in the sense of explicitly thematizing them. The assumption that a public sphere can overlook, bracket, or disregard social and cultural differences is counterfactual. Fraser argues:

> In stratified societies, unequally empowered social groups tend to develop unequally valued cultural styles. The result is the development of powerful informal pressures that marginalize the contributions of members of subordinated groups both in everyday contexts and in official public spheres. Moreover, these pressures are amplified, rather than mitigated, by the particular political economy of the bourgeois public sphere. In this public sphere the media that constitute the material support for the circulation of views are privately owned and operated for profit. Consequently, subordinated social groups usually lack equal access to the material means of equal participation. (120)

If we take these considerations seriously, we should also doubt any conception of the public sphere that purports to bracket social inequalities. We should question whether it is even possible for constituents to deliberate as if they were equals in a discursive arena that is situated in a larger societal context of hierarchy and stratification. Therefore, the bourgeois conception of the public sphere "is inadequate insofar as it supposes that social equality is not a necessary condition for participatory parity in public spheres" (121).

Fraser's second critique of the Habermasian bourgeois public sphere is that it as-sumes that a single, comprehensive public sphere is closer to a true democracy than the proliferation of a multiplicity of competing publics. Habermas's account stresses the singularity of the bourgeois conception of the public sphere, and he also tends to assert the virtues of that conception. Fraser, on the other hand, contends that "in strati-fied societies, arrangements that accommodate contestation among a plurality of competing publics better promote the ideal of participatory parity than does a single, comprehensive, overarching public" (122). Since it is not possible to bracket social dif-ferences in a single public sphere, it stands to reason that it would be advantageous for marginalized groups and individuals to create public spheres where they could meet with others like them.

Similar to Negt and Kluge's conception of *proletarian public spheres,* Fraser asserts the importance of what she calls *subaltern counterpublics:* alternative public spheres consisting of subordinated social groups. These subaltern counterpublics have, in the past, consisted of women, workers, people of color, and gays and lesbians. Fraser suggests that perhaps the most striking example of this is the "late twentieth century U.S. feminist subaltern counterpublic, with its variegated array of journals, bookstores, publishing companies, film and video distribution networks, lecture series, research centers, academic programs, conferences, conventions, festivals, and local meeting places" (123).

While these counterpublics are not necessarily virtuous or democratic, they do arise in response to exclusions within dominant publics and help to expand discursive space. Fraser writes that "in general, the proliferation of subaltern counterpublics means a widening of discursive contestation, and that is a good thing in stratified societies" (124). She suggests that in stratified societies, subaltern counterpublics have a dual character. On the one hand, they function as spaces of withdrawal and regroupment— an idea reminiscent of Mary Louise Pratt's notion of the "safe house." On the other hand, they also function as bases and training grounds for "agitational activities di-rected toward wider publics" (124). These two capacities enable subaltern counter-publics to partially offset, though not completely eradicate, the unjust participatory privileges enjoyed by members of dominant social groups in stratified societies. Fraser suggests that while true participatory parity is not possible in stratified societies, it is more closely approximated by arrangements that permit contestation among a plu-rality of competing publics than by a single, comprehensive public.

Fraser also critiques Habermas's assumption that discourse in public spheres should be limited to deliberation about the common good, and that the appearance of pri-vate issues and interests is always undesirable. Habermas argued that the bourgeois public sphere was a site where private persons deliberated about "public matters."

However, what the term "public" might mean is ambiguous and open to interpretation. Fraser writes:

> There are several different senses of "private" and "public" in play here. "Public," for example, can mean (1) state-related, (2) accessible to everyone, (3) of concern to everyone, and (4) pertaining to a common good or interest. Each of these corresponds to a contrasting sense of "private." (128)

In regard to the sense that the term "public" might mean "of concern to everyone," she suggests that only participants can decide what is of common concern, and there is no guarantee that all of them will agree. What will count as a matter of common concern will be decided through discursive contestation. Any consensus that has been reached through such contestation will have been "reached through deliberative processes tainted by the effects of dominance and subordination" (131).

Fraser argues that the terms "public" and "private" are not simply straightforward designations of societal spheres; they are "cultural classifications and rhetorical labels" (131). As such, they function ideologically to delimit the boundaries of the public sphere in ways that disadvantage subordinate social groups. The rhetoric of "domestic privacy" excludes some interests from public debate. It casts them as private, domestic, or personal, and therefore off-limits for "public" discussion. Fraser writes that

> the result is to enclave certain matters in specialized discursive arenas and thereby to shield them from broadly based debate and contestation. This usually works to the advantage of dominant groups and individuals and to the disadvantage of their subordinates. (132)

For instance, the issue of wife battering could be labeled a "personal" or "domestic" matter and could be seen as an issue for a specialized institution such as family law or social work rather than an issue of common concern. The notions of public and private, since they are somewhat ambiguous, can be "vehicles through which gender and class disadvantages may continue to operate subtextually and informally, even after explicit, formal restrictions have been rescinded" (132).

Fraser critiques one final assumption underlying the bourgeois conception of the public sphere: that a functioning democratic public sphere requires a sharp separation between civil society and the state. Habermas suggests that the members of the bourgeois public are not state officials and their participation in the public sphere is not undertaken in any official capacity. Accordingly, their discourse does not "eventuate in binding, sovereign decisions authorizing the use of state power; on the contrary, it eventuates in public opinion" (133). He posits that the public sphere is not the state; it is the informal body of discursive opinion that can serve as a "counterweight" to the state. Thus, the bourgeois conception of the public sphere supposes that a sharp separation between civil society and the state is always desirable. Fraser suggests that this conception promotes what she calls "weak publics" whose deliberative practices only form opinions and do not encompass decision making. Fraser writes that

> the bourgeois conception seems to imply that an expansion of such publics' discursive authority to encompass decision making as well as opinion making would threaten the autonomy of public opinion, for then the public would effectively become the state, and the possibility of a critical discursive check on the state would be lost. (134)

That is, the bourgeois conception of the public sphere seems to rest on the fact that it can never have real decision-making power, as that would threaten its status as an opinion-based arena.

However, Fraser disagrees with this conception, suggesting that the force of public opinion is strengthened, not weakened, when a body representing it is empowered to translate opinion into authoritative decisions. For example, self-managing institutions such as child-care centers or residential communities could be arenas of both opinion formation and decision making. This would be "tantamount to constituting sites of direct or quasi-direct democracy, wherein all those engaged in a collective undertaking would participate in deliberations to determine its design and operation" (135). While direct democracy arrangements are not called for in some situations, she suggests that they can strengthen "weak" publics. Any conception of the public sphere that requires a sharp separation between civil society and the state will make it impossible for forms of self-management and interpublic coordination to take place.

Fraser raises some interesting questions concerning Habermas's interpretation of the bourgeois public sphere. Her study shows that the bourgeois conception of the public sphere is not adequate in a socially stratified society, if participatory parity is indeed our goal. Her theories render visible the ways in which social inequality taints deliberation, how publics are differently empowered and segmented, and how some groups and individuals are involuntarily subordinated to others.

TOWARD A NEW CONCEPTION OF THE PUBLIC SPHERE

As I have illustrated, efforts to understand the history, foundations, and internal processes of public spheres and public discourse are gaining importance in several disciplines. These efforts inform revisionist and empirical studies in sociology, history, and feminist studies; democratic theory in political science; and investigations into the impact of discourse in English studies, cultural studies, and communications. These conversations about the public sphere have been ongoing and progressive. Scholars today continue to debate what the bourgeois public sphere constituted during the seventeenth and eighteenth centuries, how some theorists idealized the democratic and emancipatory claims of the liberal public sphere, and how a new, postbourgeois model of the public sphere might be developed. I have already described the more recent but similar inquiries into public writing in composition studies. By drawing on the strengths of each of the theories of the public sphere that I have just recounted, compositionists might begin to develop a better understanding of what a "public sphere" might actually constitute, and, consequently, we might more effectively facilitate public writing in the courses we teach. At this point, I would like to outline the major contributions toward the concept of the public sphere that has been suggested by Sennett, Habermas, Negt, Kluge, and Fraser. This outline will serve as the basis for a more extended theoretical investigation of the importance of such theories for current and future discussions of public writing in composition studies. That is, by noting the contributions to the concept of the public sphere by the theorists I have mentioned, I hope to provide the framework for my conception of public writing that follows in chapter 4.

Through a careful investigation of the work of theorists such as Richard Sennett, Jürgen Habermas, Oskar Negt, Alexander Kluge, and Nancy Fraser, compositionists might begin to make important theoretical and pedagogical advancements toward a more holistic and sophisticated approach to public writing. While these are by no means the only scholars and theorists interested in the concept of the public sphere, they are among the most significant, compelling, and highly cited individuals writing about this important subject today. Only by drawing upon the insights, understandings, and speculations of each of them can we ascertain what the concept of "the public sphere" might actually entail.

From Richard Sennett, we learn that the history of the words "public" and "private" in Western culture derives from a specific social and cultural milieu and that, in fact, their first usages coincide with the fall of monarchy rule. Recognizing that the chronology of these two words is enmeshed with their historical, cultural, and political manifestations is an important concept—particularly for compositionists. As scholars of discourse, it is important for us to recognize not only that words and their meanings change in response to historical phenomena but also that words are often the very *sources* of cultural and historical changes. Obviously, discourse has been a very important tool in the evolution of the concept of the public sphere.

Sennett enables us to establish a clearer understanding of the complex social, historical, and cultural factors that contributed to the emergence of the bourgeois public sphere. He explores the events that led to the formation of the bourgeois public sphere, how he understands its growth and expansion as an arena of real political power and influence, and what he supposes are the causes and contributing factors that led to its decline in modern society. All too often, scholars fail to look at the events that have led to our current conceptions of a topic. Most of the scholars in composition who have discussed the public sphere and public writing have failed to take into account the historical implications of the concept. Only by thoroughly understanding the history of the public sphere can we hope to develop new models of it. While Sennett offers a somewhat bleak view of the public sphere today and suggests no theory or theories that might enable us to develop new models of the public sphere in the future, his work is important for its historical analysis of the changing styles of personal and public expression.

Like Sennett, Habermas's work is largely historical, and it reconfirms the importance of understanding the chronology of the concept of the public sphere. Habermas's *Structural Transformation* is perhaps the most influential and widely cited book about the public sphere, and there are a number of important notions that we might draw from it. Primarily, we can see his work as forming the fundamental definitions of what constitutes a public sphere. Obviously, his work has been both astoundingly fruitful, nearly indispensable in any discussion on the topic, and deeply problematic, the object of extensive criticism. He defines the public sphere as "a political public of private persons reasoning publicly, [in order] to exercise a critical function in mediating the relations between the essentially separate realms of civil society and the state" (381). Critics have questioned nearly every aspect of this definition, but nearly all of them have *begun* their discussions with it; it forms the basis for nearly any investigation of the public sphere and public discourse. We can also gather from Habermas that the public sphere is a site where the bracketing of difference is perhaps an important feature of public discourse. While this concept has also been critiqued, Habermas raises important issues about status, difference, and who gets to speak in the public sphere. Habermas also raises the question of the content of public discourse. Delineating that the content of public discourse must be of "common concern" is, as we have seen, vague, but it does help to focus future discussions. That these public forums were "in principle" inclusive is another significant feature of the public sphere that Habermas notes. Certainly any conception of the public sphere hinges upon the issue of access. Any investigation of the public sphere and public discourse must begin with the criteria that Habermas's *Structural Transformation* considers.

From Negt and Kluge we can see that we must not limit our discussions to one single conception of the public sphere. Instead, it is perhaps more fruitful and productive to envision public discourse as occurring at a variety of overlapping, often contending arenas. Also, their work might keep us from becoming too idealistic in our conceptions of public discourse—in the past or otherwise. The bracketing of difference, the principle of inclusivity, and the premise of open access, are, as Negt and Kluge suggest, often rhetorical assertions used to reproduce dominant ideology and reinforce dominant power. Negt and Kluge enable us to envision more radical, progressive notions of public discourse. They also allow us to discern the importance of the discursive construction of public spheres, a construction that gives the power of expression to the subaltern.

Nancy Fraser reaffirms the fact that public spheres could become sites for the exclusion of groups and individuals, based upon their race, class, sexual orientation, or gender. Fraser's analysis of competing public spheres moves us closer to the sort of discursive spaces we might help to create in our efforts to empower marginalized others. She urges us to pay closer attention to the ways in which deliberation can serve as a mask for domination; a message that we must take to heart if we are to extend discussions of the public sphere in useful and critical directions. We can also perceive that deliberative forums could translate opinion into authoritative decisions, as that might enable "weak" publics to gain some degree of efficacy.

In short, compositionists can learn something about the concept of the public sphere from each of these discussions, and, by drawing upon the strengths of each of them, we might develop a more specific theoretical approach to public writing. As a result, we should become more adept at facilitating critical public discourse in the writing courses that we teach. In the next chapter, I apply these social and cultural theories to the analogous work in composition studies in order to develop a more holistic, sophisticated analysis of the issue of public writing. That is, I meld these various discussions into one sustained examination of their importance to composition theorists, researchers, and instructors. In the process, I investigate the pedagogical implications of teaching public writing in order to facilitate democratic discursive practices within and outside of writing classrooms.

4

RETHINKING PUBLIC WRITING
Discourse, Civic Life, and Composition Studies

> Public spheres are not only arenas for the formation of discursive
> opinion; in addition, they are arenas for the formation and enactment of
> social identities. This means that participation is not simply a matter of
> being able to state propositional contents that are neutral with respect to
> form of expression. Rather . . . participation means being able to speak in
> one's own voice, and thereby simultaneously to construct and express
> one's own cultural identity through idiom and style.
>
> —NANCY FRASER, "Rethinking the Public Sphere"

WITHIN THE PAST few years, compositionists have begun to address both the rewards and difficulties of writing in public spheres. These discussions—and there have been quite a few in the discipline's major journals, conferences, and listservs—speak about our desire for meaningful and productive discourse about political and social issues that affect all of our lives. While there has been little agreement about how this desire might be satisfied, the term *public writing* has emerged as a common focal point. Briefly stated, public writing consists of written discourse that attempts to engage an audience of local, regional, or national groups or individuals in order to bring about progressive societal change. Such discourse *intends* to be free of any coercive constraints or forms of domination, and it hopes to influence what Habermas calls "public opinion."

This orientation toward public writing, which has recently become a more significant topic of conversation in composition studies than ever before, seems to be a logical and progressive development in the field. As I've suggested, since its emergence as an academic discipline in the 1960s and 1970s, composition gradually expanded its focus from the individual writer, to social notions of how knowledge is generated, to more political—and public—investigations of discourse. Radical scholars and teachers in the field of composition have changed our conceptions of the role of discourse in shaping society. Viewing the work of composition as a democratic enterprise, some

scholars have recently extended the focus of radical investigations to explore the political role of discourse outside of the classroom. That is, while radical theories enabled many compositionists to envision discourse as a political act, more and more
scholars today are broadening this notion to investigate sites outside of the classroom
in which discourse is generated and used. This investigation, which seems to fall into
several related categories including "public writing" and "service-learning in composition," might very well become the next dominant focal point around which the teaching of college writing is theorized and discussed. The proliferation of articles, chapters, and books regarding this subject seems to suggest that more and more scholars
are looking beyond the classroom in their investigations of discourse.

Not surprisingly, most of these discussions of public writing in composition have
focused on students—particularly those in the writing courses we teach. While composition theory has developed in sophisticated and meaningful directions over the past
forty years, it has, unlike theory in some other disciplines, nearly always been done in
an effort to make our work in the classroom more meaningful and productive. Composition is unique in that it revolves not around a particular body of knowledge, but
around the common goal of helping students use writing to improve their lives. The
project of knowledge-making in composition is deeply implicated in how teaching
practices are formed and argued for. As Joseph Harris writes in *A Teaching Subject,*
"composition is the only part of English studies which is commonly defined not in
relation to a subject *outside* of the academy (to literature, for example, or to culture
or language) but by its position *within* the curriculum—by its close involvement with
the gatekeeping first-year course in writing" (xi).

The desire for effective public writing, particularly as it is invested in students, attempts to make our teaching practices more important and worthwhile. For many
compositionists, the classroom—or more specifically, the writing course—has emerged
as a microcosm of the public sphere, as our point of contact with the "real" world out
there somewhere. This point of contact is something that distinguishes composition
from many other academic disciplines; our close and personal connections with students differentiates our work from the "merely academic" pursuits of our colleagues
down the hall. If we believe that power is entrenched in discourse and that language
is an instrumental tool in shaping knowledge and reality, we could, by extension, assume that the work that we do can have tangible, immediate implications in the world.

Rhetoricians and compositionists have turned toward public writing for a number
of reasons. Most important, such an approach gives student writing real significance;
public writing often allows students to produce meaningful discourse that has the
potential to change their lives and the lives of others. In this respect, students see public
writing as more "real" than, for example, an essay about what they did last summer

or an analysis of a particular piece of literature. Public writing can help students see the value of adopting a particular rhetorical stance, since public writing is often directed toward a particular audience who might be influenced by the student's writing.

Students often come away from a course or assignment that focuses on public writing with a better understanding of the importance of shaping the style, form, and tone of their written work in ways that might be most persuasive and compelling. In addition, public writing more easily allows students to see that language is a powerful tool for affecting change in the world. When a student's writing generates further public discussion or leads to some societal change, he or she comes to see how discourse is deeply implicated in the structures of power in a society. Obviously, public writing of this sort is something we'd all like to realize in the writing courses we teach. Unfortunately, few compositionists know where "the public" is located, and even fewer have thought in depth about what public writing might entail beyond letters to the editor of a newspaper or to their local congressman.

Even among the scholars and theorists in composition who have written about public writing there is little consensus on how we might envision or further theorize this genre. Their conceptions of public writing are as diverse as the public itself. To some composition theorists, like S. Michael Halloran and Lester Faigley, public writing necessitates a reorientation to public discourse in the ancient rhetorical tradition and an orientation to a "rhetoric of citizenship" within the writing classroom. Halloran's 1982 "Rhetoric in the American College Curriculum: The Decline of Public Discourse" was among the first to rightly assert that "we might well turn some of our attention to the discourse of public life" and in the process enable students to see themselves as "members of a body politic in which they have responsibility to form judgments and influence the judgments of others on public issues" (263–64). Similarly, Faigley's *Fragments of Rationality* suggests that the newer political awareness in composition studies has the potential to "recover a lost tradition of rhetoric in public life" (71). For other compositionists, such as Joseph Harris, the term "public" is a useful metaphor for how we might imagine the writing classroom in the 1990s and beyond. Harris argues for a "view of the classroom as a public space rather than as a kind of entry point into some imagined community of academic discourse" (*A Teaching Subject* 109).

Other theorists, including Susan Wells and Irene Ward, have examined composition's desire for efficacious public writing—especially as it is invested in students—and have theorized ways to construct pubic spheres that students might enter through discourse. Wells's "Rogue Cops and Health Care: What Do We Want from Public Writing" is perhaps the most thorough investigation of public writing; in it, she posits that "If we want more for our students than the ability to defend themselves in bureaucratic settings, we are imagining them in a public role, imagining a public space they could enter" (326). Ward's "How Democratic Can We Get?: The Internet, the Public Sphere, and Public Discourse" discusses the potential for "the Internet to become a public sphere and, hence, a forum that private individuals could use to democratically influence the state" (365).

Still others have attempted to introduce new forms of public writing into their courses through "service learning." Compositionists like Bruce Herzberg suggest that the kind of civic participation that service learning courses in composition offer can allow students to discover "real applications [for] their knowledge in the organizations they serve" and also learn that they "can use their knowledge not only to get jobs for themselves but also to help others" (308). Similarly, Ellen Cushman has argued that composition courses can increase participation in public discourse by "bridging the university and community through activism" ("The Rhetorician as an Agent of Social Change" 7).

Clearly, all of these compositionists see some value in the notion of public writing and public discourse. But just as clearly, none of them seem to be in agreement as to how we might most successfully enact public writing in a composition course. Perhaps part of the reason for this lack of agreement on what public writing constitutes is the absence of a sustained theoretical investigation of the subject. While these inquiries into public writing have generated some rudimentary discussions and definitions of the subject, none has yet put forth a careful and thorough examination of how we might envision public writing. Nearly all of the discussions regarding this subject in composition have thus far been peripheral; most have been short treatments of at most a few pages, usually situated somewhere within an article or book chapter. This chapter attempts to more fully theorize public writing in a way that will be most valuable and constructive for compositionists. It draws upon the work of noted social and cultural theorists including Richard Sennett, Jürgen Habermas, Oskar Negt, Alexander Kluge, and (particularly) Nancy Fraser, who have provided various careful studies of the concept of "the public." I apply these social and cultural theories of "the public" to the current topic of public writing in order to develop a more holistic, sophisticated analysis of the subject. In the process, I investigate the pedagogical implications of teaching public writing in order to facilitate democratic discursive practices within and outside of writing classrooms.

A NEW CONCEPTION OF PUBLIC WRITING

In order to realize the goal of developing a more comprehensive conception of public writing, we must first begin by defining it. Public writing can take on many particular facets and can be enacted through innumerable pedagogies. However, it is important to explain what public writing is *not,* or more accurately, what it is *not only.* Over the past few years, I have become more and more interested in moving beyond academic discourse in the writing courses I teach and toward more evocative and meaningful encounters with discourse outside of the classroom. Like many compositionists, I aspire to make my writing courses meaningful not just in terms of enabling students to be successful writers in their academic pursuits, nor even just in their future careers, but in their ability to speak and write discourse that will enable them to take part in the political and social spheres of American life. In other words, I want to help my students become active citizens who are capable of using language to defend themselves, voice their opinions, and take part in public debates. In my desire to realize this goal, I naturally asked a number of other writing teachers if they had done assignments or taught courses focusing on public writing. "Oh sure," was a common response, "I usually have them write a letter to the editor of their local newspaper on a current topic."

While this could *potentially* be a useful writing assignment, it does not fulfill all of the requirements of meaningful public writing. Such assignments, while they do appear in a publication that exists outside of the writing classroom, do little to cultivate the students' facility with public discourse. To begin with, the students' letters are very often generated just to fulfill the assignment. Occasionally students may come across a public issue that they are genuinely interested in, but more often than not, the issues students write about in their "letters to the editor" have little bearing on their lives outside of the classroom. Public writing consists of more than expressing your opinion about a current topic; it entails being able to make your voice heard on an issue that directly confronts or influences you. Moreover, such assignments have little effect on the world. While students may find these assignments empowering if their letters are published (as they occasionally are), very rarely do their letters result in any change or even any further discussion. Letters to the editor are one-way assignments; students put effort into writing them but get little subsequent response. As a result, these types of assignments are often counterproductive. Students come to feel that participating in "public discourse," if letters to the editor are indeed public discourse, has little effect on what happens in their world. They surmise that the public sphere is a realm where nothing actually gets accomplished—at least not by them.

If we are to create writing assignments and courses that actually do interact with "the public sphere" in meaningful ways, we must begin by analyzing and scrutinizing what public writing *should be.* At this point, I will highlight some of the most significant aspects of successful public writing in an attempt to facilitate more effective public writing assignments and courses for other compositionists. While these are by no means the only aspects we must consider in discussions of public writing, they are among the most significant. In order to more fully inquire into the complexities of this subject, I draw upon the work of a number of social and cultural theorists who have discussed the notion of the public sphere. There are many parallels between the conversations of the public sphere in social and cultural theory and the conversations in composition regarding public writing. It is my hope that this explication will enable others to rethink what public writing actually entails and, by extension, transform their thoughts into more constructive and meaningful public writing assignments and courses.

Public Writing in Context

One significant misconception of public writing has to do with the contextual/historical understandings (or lack thereof) that most writing teachers have of the subject. Some instructors teaching public writing seem to assume that "the public" is easily found, stationary, and unencumbered by political, social, and cultural forces. Public writing, for these instructors, is a relatively ahistorical activity, requiring little thought about the conditions that gave rise to the activity of public discourse or the conditions corresponding to each particular topic in the public sphere. If they consider the historical nature of public writing at all, they assume that the avenues of public writing exist in a relatively unchanging state, uninfluenced and unchanged by larger cultural factors. They assume that, if a student writes "clearly" and "logically" in a public setting, his or her message will be recognized as valid in and of itself. As a result, some writing teachers begin with incomplete conceptions of what public writing entails, and these nearly always amount to ineffective pedagogies. Effective public writing must account for the degree to which public writing exists in a historically textured sphere that is the product of innumerable social and political forces. These forces have long histories and are in a constant state of flux. If we are to fully and cogently theorize public writing, we must begin by establishing it as a complex historical category.

Perhaps the best way to conceptualize this notion is to examine the sites in which public writing occurs. The location of public discourse—labeled "the public sphere" by many theorists—has been seen as primarily a historical concept. Efforts to understand the history, foundations, and internal processes of public discourse have been central to the conversations about the public sphere in social and cultural theory. The debate on the public sphere has been influenced most deeply by Habermas's *The Structural Transformation of the Public Sphere*. It is, as Wells writes, "both deeply problematic and astoundingly fruitful" (327). Essentially, the book builds its theoretical argument largely out of the historical growth of capitalism and democracy in Britain,

France, and Germany between the seventeenth and early twentieth centuries. In his introduction, Thomas McCarthy argues that the book is "a historical-sociological account of the emergence, transformation, and disintegration of the . . . liberal public sphere that took shape in the specific historical circumstances of a developing market economy" (xi). The book envisions the public sphere as an *institutional location* where practical reason and debate arise out of material circumstances in order to promote more democratic ideals. That is, one of the most significant aspects of *Structural Transformation* is that it sees public discourse as occurring only as a *result* of a particular cultural climate.

Habermas asserts that the public sphere "is a category that is typical of an epoch" and that "we treat public sphere in general as a historical category" (xvii). Similarly, Richard Sennett's *The Fall of Public Man* suggests the importance of a historical understanding of the concept of the public sphere. Sennett argues that his book attempts to "create a theory of expression in public by a process of interplay between history and theory" and that to have a clear understanding of the subject, it is necessary to examine "the social and political dimensions of the public problem as it has developed in modern society" (6). Both of these conceptions of the public sphere, and the many conversations that they have generated in social and cultural theory, see public discourse as arising from the distinct cultural conditions of capitalist and postcapitalist societies. They both suggest that public discourse occurs in the context of a particular cultural milieu.

If we agree that public discourse arises from a culture, and that social, political, and historical forces have constructed, shaped, and otherwise affected the locations, topics, and methods of public discourse, we are, in a sense, arguing that it is *ideologically interested*. That is, any understanding of public discourse as a product of a particular cultural climate must take into account the ways that ideology shapes and structures nearly every aspect of what, where, and how public discourse occurs as well as who gets to speak in public settings. Both Habermas and Sennett fail to fully recognize the degree to which ideology shapes public discourse, and their investigations are less thorough as a result. As I've mentioned, ideology is one of the most central aspects of current composition theory. By ideology I mean the understanding that ideas, knowledge, thought, and discourse are shaped and controlled by cultural contextual forces. In many ways, the study of the workings of ideology has become central to composition studies as we come to recognize that ideology is entwined in discourse. Discourse *is* ideological and ideology works through discourse; the relationship is dialectical. As James Berlin writes, ideology always brings with it "strong social and cultural reinforcement, so that what we take to exist, to have value, and to be possible seems necessary, normal, and inevitable—in the nature of things" (*Rhetoric and Real-*

ity 78). Therefore, it is imperative that we recognize that all public writing, and the public spheres in which it occurs, is ideologically constructed.

Berlin also notes the degree to which all discourse is shaped by the historical and ideological conditions of the culture in which it exists. He argues that experiences and expressions of material life are always mediated by the signifying practices of discourse. Since discourse is embroiled with ideology in a dialectical relationship, it follows that our experiences and expressions (be they in public or in private) are necessarily influenced by ideology. Berlin suggests that

> only through language do we know and act upon the conditions of our experience—conditions that are socially constructed, again through the agency of discourse. Ways of living and dying are finally negotiated through historically and culturally specific signifying practices, the semiotic codes of time and place. The economic, social, and political conditions of a historical period can be known and acted upon only through the discourses of the moment. (71–72)

Berlin argues here that all discourse, all writing must be seen as a historically and culturally specific practice. I would argue that in theorizing and examining the practice of public writing it is perhaps even more obvious that discourse is historically and culturally specific. If we are to fully theorize public writing, we must begin by seeing how it is shaped and transformed by forces including the social, economic, political, cultural, and ideological. By exposing these forces, both in theory and in the classroom, we arrive at a fuller understanding of what public writing is and how it works or fails to work in specific circumstances. Public writing, like any study of discourse, must be "historically specific in its methods and materials, never resting secure in any transhistorical and universal mode of thought" (76).

We must understand that the particular circumstances that produced public spheres also produced each of the particular aspects of the discourse that exists in these spheres. Recognizing that public discourse is often a reflection of the cultural climate in which it arose enables us to structure our discourse accordingly. This recognition consists of much more than merely recognizing the context of a particular public issue. It consists of recognizing the types of conversations that have preceded each particular instance of public discourse, the style in which arguments are presented, how interlocutors are evaluated, and what can and cannot be said in public debate. We must also recognize the degree to which ideology shapes nearly every aspect of public writing. Ideology normalizes the workings of power in public discourse. It makes it appear that what is being discussed, how it is being discussed, and who is discussing it is normal, natural, and unaffected by anything other than logic. For example, both Habermas's and Sennett's analyses of the bourgeois public sphere fail to note the degree to which dominant ideology shaped public debates, and, as a result, they both fail to account for the degree to which the discourse that occurred in this public sphere was controlled and manipulated by white property-owning males. In nearly all instances of public discourse, ideology naturalizes certain authority regimes—those of class, race, and gender, for example—and renders alternatives all but unthinkable. In short, recognizing that public discourse is historical, contextual, and ideologically influenced is an inherently rhetorical move.

Seeing public writing as a political move allows us to pay particular attention to both our audience and our subject. We recognize that the groups or individuals that we hope to persuade and possibly call to action are influenced by particular rhetorical modes and devices, and their reactions are often shaped by their prior experiences with public discourse. They may consider our public discourse more or less closely as a result of who we are and where we speak from. Furthermore, we can better conceptualize our subject if we see it as discursively constructed through a variety of previous public discussions. That is, our own conceptions of a particular topic are shaped by all of our previous encounters with it, and many of these encounters transpired in public spheres. Envisioning public writing in this way situates each public discursive moment as ideologically situated, itself an intervention in the political process. Public writing cannot deny its inescapable ideological predispositions. It cannot claim to be above ideology, a transcendent discourse that exists outside of history or culture. Like Berlin's Social-Epistemic Rhetoric, public writing, when seen from a historical/cultural perspective, contains "within it a utopian moment, a conception of the good democratic society and the good life for all of its members"(*Rhetoric and Reality* 81). Public writing must be aware of its historical contingency and of its limitations and incompleteness.

I'm certainly not suggesting that we have our students read Habermas, Sennett, or any other historical investigation of the public sphere. Nor am I suggesting that they read Berlin to learn more about the relationships between ideology and discourse. What I am suggesting is that we should help them to recognize that culture, politics, and ideology shape public conversations. We should highlight the ways in which material forces shape what gets said, who gets heard, and how these forces have structured public discourse throughout history. This can be accomplished by choosing particular cultural issues that have been discussed in the public sphere, examining what voices have been heard and acknowledged, what voices have been marginalized, silenced, or excluded, and how discourse on particular issues has changed or developed as a result of the larger political and social climates in which they've been generated. Students are able to easily transfer these heuristics and skills to their own areas of interest, and, as a result, they are much more capable of generating effective public writing. By looking at public writing in context, we allow students to see how to use the tools of language to their best interests and in the process discover how textual production—such as public writing—helps to shape and construct knowledge rather than simply reproduce it. Such an approach will necessitate that writers research the histories of the issues they choose to address to find out how the conversations surrounding them have been shaped, altered, and constructed. At the same time, they will need to consider what is *not* said, whose voices have been excluded from the conversation, and how ideology has normalized certain features of the public discussion they're entering.

A course or assignment focusing on public writing would need to consider how a particular issue—school vouchers, for example—has been shaped by the long history of educational debate in this country. Writers would need to consider how legislative programs such as school segregation, busing, and standardized testing have been used in the past to justify the ideological perspectives of those in power. In addition, writers would need to consider what sorts of rhetoric might open up or foreclose further discussion from various groups in the public sphere. For service learning courses such as those advocated by Bruce Herzberg, Linda Flower, and others, the particular topics of their projects would need to be considered in context. A service learning course focusing on community literacy, for example, would need to consider the particular environments in which the writers' work would take place and how the histories of literacy in various forms has already shaped those communities. These service learning projects would also need to consider how ideology, racism, classism, and sexism have played significant roles in shaping the literate practices of the individuals the students intend to tutor. Students would need to think about whether or not certain classes or races have been historically disadvantaged by their lack of "standard" literacy and how ideology and hegemony have contributed to this disadvantage. Regardless of the form or topic of the assignment or course, effective public writing necessitates a thorough investigation of the political, social, economic, cultural, and ideological forces that have influenced any public issue.

The Bracketing of Difference in Public Writing

Another significant misconception of public writing is that such writing, if done "clearly and logically," frees the individual of his or her particular ethnic, gender, or class distinctions. Public writing is often assumed to be evaluated for its merits alone, disengaged and independent from the features and characteristics of its author. Furthermore, the audience of public writing is often assumed to be composed of neutral, open-minded individuals who evaluate public discourse entirely on the merits of its argument. If, writers can only express themselves with complete clarity and grammatical and mechanical correctness, some might argue, their position will be accepted magnanimously, or at least evaluated honestly. The social inequalities that exist in the rest of society are often assumed to be set aside in the arenas of public discourse. In other words, it is often assumed that the differences and inequalities between the author of a piece of public writing and his or her audience are bracketed. In addition, it is often supposed that all individuals—regardless of their race, class, gender, sexual inclination, or other distinguishing features—are as capable and authorized to produce public writing as anyone else. In short, public discourse is often presumed to be open and accessible to all, free of any of the social inequalities that pervade other discursive situations.

Once again, it is useful to examine the discussions of the public sphere in social and cultural theory in order to most effectively theorize this aspect of public writing. Habermas's account of the bourgeois public sphere, which stresses the claim of open access to all, runs parallel with many of the current misconceptions some writing teachers seem to have of public writing. For Habermas, the idea of open access and participatory parity is one of the central aspects of public discourse. Habermas's interpretation of the bourgeois public sphere was one that posits it to have been an arena where individuals would set aside "such characteristics as differences in birth and fortune and speak to one another as if they were social and economic peers" (Fraser 118). That is, Habermas assumed that a "social leveling" of all participants was an integral part of the liberal public sphere in the seventeenth and eighteenth centuries in Europe. He writes:

> [T]hey preserved a kind of social intercourse that, far from presupposing the equality of status, disregarded status altogether. The tendency replaced the celebration of rank with a tact befitting equals. The parity on whose basis alone the authority of the better argument could assert itself against that of social hierarchy . . . meant . . . the parity of "common humanity." . . . Not that this idea of the public was actually realized in earnest in the coffee houses, the salons, and the societies; but as an idea it had become institutionalized and thereby stated as an objective claim. If not realized, it was at least consequential. (*Structural Transformation* 36)

The assumption that Habermas (and some writing instructors) seems to make is that societal equality is not a necessary precondition for fair and equal public discourse. In other words, they assume that public spheres are somehow more egalitarian and democratic than the rest of society. Of course, we know from Habermas's account that the bourgeois public's claim to full accessibility and equality was not, in fact, realized—just as public discourse today is not entirely open to all and free of status differentials. The same forms of domination and control present in other realms of society are at least as pervasive, if not more so, in the realm of public discourse.

Nancy Fraser questions the assumption that it is possible for interlocutors in any public debate to actually bracket status differentials and to participate in discourse as if all of the members of a public sphere were social equals. She suggests that in the bourgeois public sphere, or any other public sphere for that matter, it is impossible to effectively bracket social differences among interlocutors. She writes:

> But were they [the differences between interlocutors] really effectively bracketed? The revisionist historiography suggests that they were not. Rather, discursive interaction within the bourgeois public sphere was governed by protocols of style and decorum that were themselves correlates and markers of status inequality. These functioned informally to marginalize women and members of the plebeian classes and to prevent them from participating as peers. (119)

In this respect, Fraser is talking about informal impediments to participatory parity that can persist even after everyone is formally and legally licensed to participate. Certainly, there are no legal restrictions on public writing in the United States today, regardless of the circumstances. Such restrictions are not allowable by law. This fact has, unfortunately, created a situation that makes public discourse *appear* to be equally open to all, existing in arenas that have overcome all social exclusions and marginalizations. However, public discourse is influenced by forces that cannot be easily disposed of through legislation. Fraser notes a number of these informal impediments to participatory parity in public discourse. She cites, for example, a familiar contemporary example drawn from feminist research. It has been documented that in mixed-sex deliberations, men tend to interrupt women more than women interrupt men; men also tend to speak more than women; and women's interventions are more often ignored or not responded to than men's. Deliberation and the appearance of participatory parity can serve as a mask for domination. Acknowledging the work of theorists like Jane Mansbridge, Fraser argues that various manipulations of discourse are often used to cloak nearly imperceptible modes of control. Fraser argues that

> the transformation of "I" into "we" brought about through political deliberation can easily mask subtle forms of control. Even the language people use as they reason together usually favors one way of seeing things and discourages

others. Subordinate groups sometimes cannot find the right voice or words to express their thoughts, and when they do, they discover they are not heard. [They] are silenced, encouraged to keep their wants inchoate, and heard to say "yes" when what they have said is "no." (119)

Many of these feminist insights into ways that discourse is used to mask domination and imbalances of power can be applied to other kinds of unequal relations, like those based on class or ethnicity. They alert us to the ways in which "social inequalities can infect deliberation, even in the absence of any formal exclusions" (119). In this respect, the bracketing of differences and social inequalities in public discourse cannot actually be enacted, and making the assumption that such bracketing can be enacted actually works to the advantage of dominant groups in a public sphere and to the disadvantage of subordinates. In most cases, it would be more appropriate to *unbracket* these inequalities by foregrounding and thematizing them. Doing this would help to eliminate some of the more pernicious uses of discourse in public deliberation. The assumption that public writing occurs in an arena that can overlook, bracket, or disregard social and cultural differences is counterfactual.

In composition studies, Evelyn Ashton-Jones and a number of other scholars have noted similar studies in their investigations of the ways in which social differences affect discursive situations. Like Fraser, Ashton-Jones argues that social factors—and she uses gender differences as just one example—often radically influence the dynamics of a discursive situation and determine whether and how an individual's voice is heard or interpreted. She suggests that the studies of conversational dynamics prove that discursive interaction is largely controlled by the ideology of gender, and these conversational events are no less distinct in group writing situations. She argues:

> On the contrary, it is more likely that in writing groups women's and men's behavior will parallel the conversational events described in these studies, men interacting as the individualists pressing to get across their point of view—thus controlling the realities produced in these writing communities—and women shouldering the major share of the necessary interactional work. (16)

There is no reason to think that these conversational dynamics are somehow miraculously absent from the particular discursive situation of public writing. On the contrary, since public discourse often brings together individuals from radically different perspectives and positions, and since these individuals often have no prior bonds or other incentives that would urge them to work toward participatory parity, it stands to reason that these status differentials are perhaps even more apparent and significant in public settings. In fact, not even a clear predominance of power and status in favor of women (or other marginalized groups) accords them participatory parity. Ashton-Jones suggests that women and men are consigned, by virtue of gender, to gender-specific interactive styles, their options foreclosed in advance of any conversational encounter. The ideology of gender, like the ideologies of race and class, constructs and reconstructs all sorts of discursive interaction. The imbalances of power that exist in nearly every aspect of society are not likely to disappear magically when the scene of meaning making shifts to public writing. The studies that both Fraser and Ashton-Jones cite and support suggest that public writing is simply one more example of a microinstitution in which patterns of dominance based upon race, class, or gender are reproduced, yet another stage on which the ideologies of race, class, and gender are played out (Ashton-Jones 17).

For communicative situations such as public writing, gender-specific power differences cannot be disregarded. In fact, any course or assignment focusing on public writing must recognize the degree to which a number of other social forces—among them race, ethnicity, sexual orientation, age, occupation, class—influence the idealized, status-free public spheres envisioned by some writing instructors. Compositionists must recognize that social differences shape public writing in significant ways. We also need to continue efforts to establish new theories of public writing that acknowledge differences in thinking and writing. At the same time, we need to be careful that these theories address the origins of many of these differences as ideologically constructed. As such, the label "difference" must be seen as a term that can be used to reinforce and justify marginal or dominant status.

In composition courses focusing on public writing, it is important to highlight for students the degree to which their social status and differences from others will affect how their writing is evaluated. They will also need to examine how differences themselves are often labels that are used to justify the dominance or subordination of certain classes or groups in public settings. Students will need to question whether it is possible, even in principle, for individuals to deliberate through public discourse as if they were social peers. If public discourse is situated in a larger societal context that is pervaded by structural relations of dominance and subordination—and students will be the first to note these societal differences—it must follow that public writing will not be evaluated free of these systemic inequalities. In addition, it is also important to enable student writers to examine the ways that they themselves often evaluate the public discourse of others in similarly biased and unproductive ways. Keeping in mind the fact that inequalities are a very real and significant aspect of public writing allows students to be more perceptive and discerning of the discourse they consume and produce. One task of an effective public writing assignment is to render visible the ways that societal inequality infects formally inclusive existing public spheres and taints discursive interaction within them.

Multiple Spheres for Public Writing

Some writing teachers who implement public writing assignments seem to assume that there is just one significant site for public writing, just one arena where an individual's voice might be heard: the local newspaper. Some of the instructors I have spoken with about public writing assignments suppose that the only meaningful avenue for student public writing lies in letters sent to a local newspaper (usually directed to the editor) that may or may not result in publication somewhere deep inside the daily or weekly edition of the news. When questioned about this belief, many respond that the newspaper is the only site available to students to reach a wide audience of diverse individuals who might be interested in what these students have to say. They argue that student public discourse is only worthwhile if it reaches a large segment of the population who are able to act upon it in some way. Furthermore, they suggest that public writing must address an eclectic audience, since addressing an assorted constituency is the only way that students can learn to deliberate effectively with diverse groups and individuals. In other words, it is often assumed that public writing must address the "general public," and the term *public* is often taken to encompass all members of a society, or at least a representative microcosm of them. There are three significant flaws in the thinking behind this belief. First, it is incorrect to assume that newspapers are the only significant medium for reaching others through public writing. Second, public writing need not reach large segments of the population in order to be useful and constructive. Third, there is no reason to suppose that public writing must be directed to a diverse audience. By turning to the work of Habermas, Negt, Kluge, and Fraser, I will explain why these assumptions are faulty and how we might more productively envision this aspect of public writing.

The belief that a large audience is mandatory for public writing, and that this audience must represent all or many of the types of individuals in a society, runs parallel with some of Habermas's conceptions of the public sphere. Habermas's account stresses the singularity of the bourgeois conception of the public sphere, its claim to be *the* public arena, in the singular. Habermas asserts that the bourgeoisie in seventeenth- and eighteenth-century Europe conceived of "the public sphere as something properly theirs" (24). His narrative seems to agree with this conception, since it "casts the emergence of additional publics as a late development signaling fragmentation and decline" (Fraser 122). That is, Habermas seems to suggest that any departure from this conception of a singular public sphere is a departure from the ideal. Like the conceptions of public writing I've just mentioned, Habermas's narrative is based upon an underlying assumption: that confining public discourse to a single, overarching public sphere is a desirable and positive move, whereas the proliferation of discourse in a multiplicity of public spaces represents a departure from, rather than an advance toward, democracy.

In contrast to Habermas, Negt and Kluge's *Public Sphere and Experience* insists on the need to understand postbourgeois public formations in terms other than those of disintegration and decline. In fact, they assert that no singular form of the public did or ever could exist. They understand public discourse as existing in numerous sites that have "no homogeneous substance whatsoever" (13). In their attempt to make sense of this absence of a single, overarching public sphere, Negt and Kluge suggest that there are at least two other significant arenas of public discourse: the "public sphere of production," which is more directly rooted in the spheres of capitalism such as factory communities and labor unions, and the "proletarian public sphere," which is "substantively meshed with the history of the emancipation of the working class" (xliv). Moreover, Negt and Kluge make the point that these other sites for public discourse cannot be viewed in isolation from one another; these public spheres must be seen as "mutually imbricated," overlapping, cohabitational, and often contradictory. In contrast to the conception that there must be one singular site of public discourse, and that it must consist of a diverse public, Negt and Kluge suggest that there are multiple arenas for public discourse, and these might best serve the needs of particular groups, rather than a general public.

Nancy Fraser's analysis of this misconception is equally compelling. Counter to Habermas's confidence in an all-encompassing site for public discourse that is comprised of a cross-section of society, Fraser contends that in stratified societies, "arrangements that accommodate contestation among a plurality of competing publics better promote the ideal of participatory parity than does a single, comprehensive, overarching public" (122). As I have explained earlier, she suggests that in societies whose basic structure generates unequal social groups in relations of dominance and subordination (such as the United States), full parity of participation in public discourse is not feasible. Despite the fact that all members of a society may be *allowed* to participate in public discourse, it is impossible to insulate special discursive arenas from the effects of societal inequality. This being the case, she goes on to assert that the disadvantages these marginalized groups face are only exacerbated where there is only one single arena for public discourse. If there were only one site for public discourse, members of subordinate groups would have no arenas for deliberation among themselves about their needs, objectives, and strategies. They would have no "venues in which to undertake communicative processes that were not, as it were, under the su-

pervision of dominant groups" (123). In other words, if there were only a single public sphere, subaltern groups would have no discursive spaces in which to deliberate
free of oppression.

Fraser suggests that it is advantageous for subordinated groups to constitute alternative sites of public discourse—what she calls *subaltern counterpublics*. She envisions
these sites as "parallel discursive arenas where members of subordinated social groups
invent and circulate counterdiscourses to formulate oppositional interpretations of
their identities, interests, and needs" (123). Perhaps the most striking example of a
subaltern counterpublic in contemporary history is the late twentieth-century U.S.
feminist subaltern counterpublic, with its diverse array of journals, bookstores, publishing companies, film and video distribution networks, lecture series, research centers, academic programs, conferences, conventions, festivals, and local meeting places
(123). While subaltern counterpublics are not always inherently democratic or progressive, they do emerge in response to exclusions and omissions within dominant publics, and, as such, they help expand discursive space. In general, the proliferation of
subaltern counterpublics means a widening of discursive contestation, and "that is
a good thing in stratified societies" (124). Subaltern counterpublics can serve at least
two functions. On the one hand, they function as spaces where oppressed others can
withdraw, regroup, and heal; on the other hand, they function as "training grounds"
and bases for the development of discourse or action that might agitate or disrupt
wider publics.

Several scholars in composition have noted the usefulness of employing alternative or subaltern arenas for public writing. Susan Wells argues that compositionists
"need to build, or take part in building public spheres that . . . cannot, in our society
be unitary" (326). She goes on to suggest that given the intractable fragmentation of
modern society, the representations of the public we offer students "beyond the classroom will be provisional; we will look for alternate publics and counter publics" (335).
Wells offers a number of possible alternative publics we might engage with through
public writing assignments, including paired writing classes at different institutions,
the collection of oral histories, and the establishment of computer-networked classes.
Similarly, Irene Ward explores the potential for the Internet to become an alternative
public sphere. While she rightly addresses the many problems with employing the
Internet for public writing, she does suggest that "some forms of the Internet, perhaps the World Wide Web, can potentially function in ways that print media functioned
in the eighteenth century by delivering information, points of view, and extended
argument to a growing sector of the public" (375). Many of the service-learning approaches that Bruce Herzberg, Linda Flower, and others advocate form counterpublics
through public writing. Adult literacy programs form alternative arenas for public

discourse by "linking courses with community agencies" in an effort to make students "better citizens, citizens in the strongest sense of those who take responsibility for communal welfare" (Herzberg 66).

Obviously, public writing need not be limited to a single discursive arena like a newspaper. As compositionists, it should be our responsibility to help students discover the various counterpublics where their public writing might have a receptive audience and, consequently, might result in significant outcomes. Public writing is never a matter of simply writing clearly and effectively in order to persuade or inform. Public discourse is often difficult to generate and often even more difficult to disseminate to particular audiences. Compositionists should work to create spaces for public writing if they don't exist or aren't readily entered by students. Public writing can exist in a number of sites. Often, students feel most comfortable joining in conversation in Internet chat rooms, volunteer organizations, community outreach programs, or other smaller venues that target more specific issues and strive for and generate significant local results. Rather than feeling that they are just a few small individuals who are unable to bring about sweeping changes—as is usually the case with letters to a newspaper with a wide circulation—students working with smaller, more specific groups often see tangible results from their public discourse.

In addition, public writing does not necessarily need to address a diverse audience. In fact, student discourse is often most effective if it is aimed at individuals who share common perspectives and goals. Enabling students to connect with counterpublics comprised of like-minded individuals is an important component of a successful public writing assignment or course. In specific counterpublics, students often find that they can generate effective public discourse in a climate that is supportive and nurturing, which prepares them to enter larger public debates in the future. Also, these counterpublics allow them to see that they don't necessarily stand alone in their views and opinions, and they learn from others with similar experiences and perspectives and often come away from such interactions with more complex and sophisticated views on public topics. Entering into discourse with specific counterpublics is often the most effective way for students to enter public space, and this move can encourage students to feel that public discourse is worth pursuing in the future.

Public Writing and Common Concerns

An additional significant misconception of public writing must be debunked if we are to theorize and teach public writing more competently and productively: the misunderstanding that public writing must be confined to matters of "common concern" to all of the members in a society. Similar to the last misconception that I addressed, this fallacy assumes that the topic of public discourse must affect all (or at least many) members of society. Such thinking supposes that by definition public writing must deal with the public in general and cannot be confined to matters of specific or particular interest. This belief often results from dualistic thinking, which juxtaposes "public" with its apparent opposite, "private." It is easy to see how issues are often placed into either of these two categories. If a topic does not seem to affect a large segment of the public, it is easily relegated to the realm of the private, and as such it is not seen as an appropriate topic for public writing. Students who choose to write about issues that do not appear to concern large segments of the population might be chastised for shortsighted, myopic thinking and encouraged to address topics that have wider implications and audiences. However, as I shall show, the myth that matters must be of "common concern" to be considered viable topics for public writing is based upon an ideologically interested notion of what counts as public matter.

Habermas suggests that the bourgeois public sphere was to be a discursive arena in which "private persons" deliberated about "public matters." He argues that discussion within this public sphere was grounded on the idea that areas that had previously been off-limits were now problematized and questioned. At first, this took the form of bourgeois discussions of the merits of art, music, and literature—subjects that had previously been confined to aristocrats and noblemen. Gradually, the commodification of cultural products made them more accessible to the public, taking them out of the control of the church and state. Habermas writes that

> discussion within such a public presupposed the problematization of areas that until then had not been questioned. The domain of "common concern" which was the object of public critical attention remained a preserve in which church and state authorities had the monopoly of interpretation not just from the pulpit but in philosophy, literature, and art, even at a time when, for specific social categories, the development of capitalism already demanded a behavior whose rational orientation required ever more information. To the degree, however, to which philosophical and literary works and works of art in general were produced for the market and distributed through it, these culture products became similar to that type of information: as commodities they became in principle generally accessible. (*Structural Transformation* 36)

Over time, these public discussions of "common concerns" came to include not just art, literature, and philosophy, but economics and politics as well. As Ward writes, "those who were interested could and did interpret works of art, literature, philosophy, and even economic and political texts through conversations at the societies, salons, and coffee houses, and in the popular press" (371–72). In short, the interpretation of matters of common interest was open to a much broader segment of society.

Fraser critiques Habermas's assumption that discourse in public spheres should be limited to deliberation about the common good, and that the appearance of private issues and interests is always undesirable. What Habermas and some teachers of public writing seem to argue is that public spheres must be sites where private persons deliberate about "public matters." However, what they fail to recognize is that the term "public" is ambiguous and open to interpretation. Fraser argues that there are several usages of the term "public," and in regard to the sense that the term might mean "of concern to everyone," she suggests that only participants can decide what is of common concern, and there is no guarantee that all of them will agree. Fraser suggests that the term "public" is "ambiguous between what objectively affects or has an impact on everyone as seen from an outsider's perspective, and what is recognized as a matter of common concern by participants" (128–29). Only participants can decide what is of common concern to them. However, there is no guarantee that they will all agree, and what will actually count as a matter of common concern will be decided through discursive contestation. Any consensus that has been reached through such contestation will have been reached "through deliberative processes tainted by the effects of dominance and subordination" (131). In other words, those who are in power get to decide what is a public issue and what is not.

Fraser asserts that the terms "public" and "private" are not simply straightforward designations of societal spheres; they are "cultural classifications and rhetorical labels" (131). As such, they function ideologically to delimit the boundaries of public discourse to the disadvantage of subordinate groups and individuals. For example, the issue of domestic violence was, until quite recently, considered to be a private matter between what was assumed to be a fairly small number of heterosexual couples. Feminists were in the minority in thinking that "domestic violence against women was a matter of common concern and thus a legitimate topic of public discourse" (129). The feminist counterpublic, however, was instrumental in disseminating a view of domestic violence as a widespread systemic feature of male-dominated societies. Only through their sustained discursive contestation were they able to make it a matter of common concern.

As teachers of public writing, it is crucial that we help students look at how the labeling of some interests as "public" and others as "private" is an ideological mystification. Matters that have heretofore been labeled private—such as sexual orientation, spousal and acquaintance abuse, and other matters of domestic or personal life—need to brought into public discourse by students. It is our responsibility to enable students to discover and write about all of the issues that affect their lives—not just those that have been delegated "of common concern." In general, composition needs to take a

more critical look at what we have determined are matters of public or private interest, and we must be willing to engage with issues that are often disturbing and unpleas-
ant. We should begin by highlighting how the notions of public and private can be
vehicles through which race, class, and gender disadvantages operate subtextually and
informally, even after formal restrictions have been removed.

Public Writing, Decision Making, and Action

There is one final assumption about public writing that I would like to address: that
its only purpose is to sway public opinion and that it does not encompass actual decision making and action. Some instructors of public writing who employ newspapers
as their primary avenue for such assignments seem to feel that students' public writing can rarely lead to substantial changes in public policy and can at best only convince
others to "think differently." While many instructors *hope* that public writing might
change society, they do not see the role of such discourse as a primary agent in social
change; any results that come from public writing are secondary, resulting well after
sustained public debate. This presumption is especially pernicious because it forecloses
real results from student writing and often turns public writing assignments into pointless and futile exercises. While I'm not suggesting that public writing must *always* lead
to decision making, I do believe that in certain circumstances it can. As I will explain,
public writing can form opinions *and* translate them into authoritative decisions, but
only if we reconsider the presumption that public discourse is necessarily separated
from legislative action.

Interestingly, Habermas suggests that a fundamental aspect of a functioning democratic public sphere is that it requires a sharp separation between civil society (the
public) and the state (the government). He stops short of recognizing the power manifested in the bourgeois public sphere, in particular, and suggests that there was no
immediate implementation of the opinions produced through this sphere's deliberations. He notes that the bourgeois public *"readied* themselves to *compel* public authority" (*Structural Transformation* 27). This definition delineates the public sphere not as
a site for the compulsion itself, but only for readying oneself to compel. Even that
compulsion, had it been realized, was only a compulsion for the authorities to engage
in further dialogue. Habermas suggests that the members of the bourgeois public were
not (and could not be) state officials and their participation in the public sphere was
not undertaken in any official capacity. Accordingly, as Fraser notes, Habermas's conception of public discourse does not "eventuate in binding, sovereign decisions authorizing the use of state power; on the contrary, it eventuates in public opinion" (133).
Seen from this perspective, the public sphere is the polar opposite of the state; it is the

informal body of discursive opinion that can serve as a "counterweight" to the state. It cannot make formal decisions on public issues because its scope is limited to conjecture, speculation, and debate about public matters. It is precisely this aspect of the public sphere that confers an aura of legitimacy, impartiality, and independence on the "public opinion" formed within it. Thus, Habermas's conception of the public sphere supposes that a sharp separation between civil society and the state is always desirable.

However, Fraser disagrees with this conception, arguing that the force of public opinion is strengthened, not weakened, when a body representing it is empowered to translate opinion into authoritative decisions. For example, self-governing institutions such as child-care centers, self-managed workplaces, or residential communities can be arenas of both opinion formation and decision making. She suggests that in these *strong publics,* whose discourse encompasses both deliberation and action, the "force of public opinion is strengthened when a body representing it is empowered to translate such 'opinion' into authoritative decisions" (134–35). The formation of these strong publics would be "tantamount to constituting sites of direct or quasi-direct democracy, wherein all those engaged in a collective undertaking would participate in deliberations to determine its design and operation" (135). While these internal public spheres would still be accountable to a larger public in many respects, their mere existence is a step toward a more egalitarian society, since they disseminate authority and power to a greater number of publics and individuals.

Students' public writing can have significant, tangible, immediate results if it is directed toward publics where both debate *and* decision making are central goals. As facilitators of public writing, it is important that we help students locate strong publics where their voices can lead to action. Asking students to write in spheres where discourse does not often lead to direct action, such as the local newspaper, is often pointless and futile. There are many arenas where student discourse can lead to palpable changes for them and others, and students may very well be members of these publics already. Students are often involved and engaged in student governments, campus organizations, resident-life committees, and workplace unions before they enroll in composition courses, and these and others are certainly sites where their discourse can have significant effects. We should encourage students to write for publics where their discourse can have real import, and we should help them to develop the rhetorical skills they will need to sway opinion and bring about change.

A PUBLIC WRITING PEDAGOGY

These are just a few of the important aspects of public writing that should be considered in the move to make student discourse more meaningful and effective. There are certainly other questions to be addressed as compositionists investigate this sometimes difficult but often tremendously rewarding approach to writing instruction. I'm not suggesting that letters to the editor *cannot* be meaningful and rewarding, only that there are other forms of public discourse, other ways of seeing the importance of discourse in the world, other sites for students to enter discursively, and other considerations that must be addressed if we hope to effectively facilitate students' entrance into the discourse of civic life.

Examples of effective public writing courses and assignments are proliferating across disciplines and across the United States. In fact, they have been for some time. A particularly useful example is found in Susan Miller's "Cross-Curricular Underlife: A Collaborative Report on Ways with Academic Words," written in collaboration with five undergraduate students. The article describes their investigations of local variations and multiple discourse communities across the academic spectrum. Through their study, students learned that "the relation between any language process and learning . . . differs, in important ways, from the single image of academic literacy" often promoted in college-level writing courses (11). The course emphasized the ability to "adapt to uses of language in new settings" and emphasized "finding variations among discourse communities"—skills that are at the heart of effective public writing (27). What is perhaps most interesting about Miller's course is the article itself. Coauthored with the students that are its very subject, it is at once an analysis and an example of discourse that transcends the isolated writing classroom. By facilitating students' examinations of discourse across disciplines and promoting those examinations through their coauthored essay, Miller's students come to understand that discourse exists in a variety of sites, and that careful attention to the variations of each particular community will enable more effective discourse.

At this point, I'd like to explain briefly how I've put some of these principles of public writing into practice in a writing course of my own. In the fall semester of 1999, I taught an Advanced Composition course entitled, "Environmental Discourse and Public Writing." The course addressed local, national, and global environmental issues in contemporary society; the causes and origins of many of the most pressing environmental problems; and how these problems have been addressed through public discourse in the media, political debates, popular culture, and other public arenas. The course had several goals: to raise student awareness of environmental problems, to help students to become "environmentally literate," and, perhaps most importantly, to enable students to voice their own opinions and bring about environmental change through public discourse. While this is just one of many topics around which to organize a course focusing on public writing, it is one that was extremely successful for my students and me.

Aside from being one of the most pressing and important issues in the world today, the environment is also one of the most widely debated and contentious issues in the public sphere. My students had no trouble selecting issues to research and write about, and they were quick to discover that these problems affect all of society and are not specific to any particular group. We began the semester by discussing the relationship between discourse and environment, underscoring the fact that while environmental problems do indeed exist, what we think, say, and do about environmental degradation is largely determined through discourse—much of which is generated in public arenas. The class came to see the environment as a concept and an associated set of cultural values that we have constructed through the way we use language. Two books were instrumental in highlighting this fact: Herndl and Brown's *Green Culture* and Killingsworth and Palmer's *Ecospeak*. Both books emphasize the rhetorical nature of all public discourse—particularly that dealing with the natural world. The recognition that public discourse is not merely the "clear" articulation of facts allowed students to be much more critical in their interpretations of public discourse.

After our introductory discussions about the rhetorical nature of environmental discourse in the public sphere, we looked into the history of environmental writing in the United States. After reading selections by authors such as Thoreau, Muir, and Leopold, students were quick to note that Nature writing in the United States began with an individualistic, masculinist bent. Later in the semester, they noted the remnants of this perspective in current environmental writing—coming from authors of various environmental perspectives. Similarly, while reading selections by authors like Rachel Carson, Annie Dillard, and Terry Tempest Williams, students became more aware of the degree to which gender and other factors influenced what these authors wrote as well as how their writing was construed in public spheres as a result of these social factors. By reading critiques of these authors' works, students began to see how an author's race, class, or gender affects how their discourse is perceived by particular publics. Many students were drawn to Al Gore's introduction to *Silent Spring,* in which he writes:

> The attack on Rachel Carson has been compared to the bitter assault on
> Charles Darwin when he published *The Origin of Species.* Moreover, because
> Carson was a woman, much of the criticism directed at her played on stereo-
> types of her sex. Calling her "hysterical" fit the bill exactly. *Time* magazine
> added the charge that she had used "emotion-fanning" words. She was
> dismissed by others as a "priestess of nature." Her credibility as a scientist was
> attacked as well: opponents financed the production of propaganda that
> supposedly refuted her work. It was all part of an intense, well-financed

negative campaign, not against a political candidate but against a book and its author. (xvi)

Reading these and other selections provided students with the background they would need to speak with the authority and competence necessary to enter public discourse about the environment. Moreover, they learned that public discourse is often not easily entered, is often laden with stereotypes and prejudices, and often reflects many of the inequalities of the society in which it exists. From these historical readings, many students recognized that social, political, and historical forces construct and shape public discourse about the environment—as they do all public discourse.

After students developed a familiarity with public discourse, they were encouraged, through several assignments, to attempt to generate their own public discourse on environmental issues that affected or interested them. I encouraged them to turn to specific arenas of public discourse, and we spent a significant amount of time discussing some of these arenas. While some students chose to write letters to the local newspaper or letters to their congressional representative, most found distinct counterpublics in which to write. These ranged from articles written for environmental activist groups such as Greenpeace, to interviews with local developers, contractors, and builders. In these arenas, students examined specific issues, some of which might have been deemed "private interests" by larger publics. For example, one student wrote a detailed report on environmentally friendly landscaping techniques, which he delivered to the developers of several nearby apartment buildings. Some students chose to use their knowledge and skills in ways that closely resembled the service learning approaches advocated by some compositionists. Several, for example, volunteered as writers for environmental organizations and were able to use their writing abilities in the production of newsletters, mailers, and other forms of counterpublic discourse. In fact, one student was able to obtain a job with the Environmental Protection Agency as a result of her volunteer work. While quite a few of the students' writings were published in some public arena outside of the classroom, we also looked at our particular group as its own public space. Consequently, we collected samples of each student's best work and published them in a classroom journal and on the Internet.

Through the course, students seemed to develop a critical awareness of the rhetoric of environmental issues, how environmental discourse has been shaped by social and historical forces, and the role of ideology in shaping our understandings of the relationship between humans and the natural world. In addition, they became more comfortable with various public spheres, learning how to transform their own personal strengths and perspectives into both decision making and tangible action. A course in pubic writing need not be organized around any particular topic; in fact, public writing is often most meaningful when each student addresses an issue of his or her choice. The various aspects of public writing that I've commented upon are contingent upon an incalculable number of circumstances; they are intended to promote more critical, and hopefully more constructive, ways of envisioning student public writing. While these suggestions certainly do not answer Susan Wells's question "What Do We Want from Public Writing?" they do, I hope, move us closer toward understanding where that question might lead.

5

ACTIVISM IN THE ACADEMY
The Compositionist as Public Intellectual

> The idea of public service must be detached from the idea of public
> monopoly, yet remain public service in the true sense. The only way of
> achieving this is to create new kinds of institutions.
> —RAYMOND WILLIAMS, *Keywords: A Vocabulary of Culture and Society*

AS I'VE SUGGESTED in previous chapters, some of the most significant and important discussions in composition studies within the past
few years have begun to examine the benefits and challenges of writing in public
spheres. These discussions address our discipline's desire for purposeful and constructive discourse about the political and social matters that affect all of our lives. Not
surprisingly, most of the discussions regarding this topic have focused almost exclusively on the discourse that students in composition courses might generate. Research
and scholarship in composition, unlike that in many other disciplines, has always
foregrounded writing instruction as its primary focus. To this end, compositionists
interested in public writing have seen the discourse produced by students in their efforts to improve their lives and the lives of others as supremely important—and rightly
so. The most significant goal of a semester's worth of writing instruction, they argue,
is or should be to help students to use language as a tool for effecting change in the
world. The composition course has emerged as both a microcosm of the public
sphere—a point of contact with the "real" world out there somewhere—as well as a
place for students to prepare for immersion into public life—a point of departure to
social and political spheres in society. As compositionists, we have come to see writing in the world "outside" our classrooms as vitally important to the lives of our students, and many writing instructors have consequently made efforts to expand classroom work to address larger audiences and broader issues. Many compositionists have
attempted to do more than have students read canonical literary texts, and their efforts have begun to enable students to focus on the political and social world as a text
to be interpreted, evaluated, and written about. Such an approach gives student writ-

ing real significance; public writing often allows students to produce work that has the potential to change their lives, the lives of their families and loved ones, and the lives of others that they care about.

While most of the discussions concerning "publicness" in composition studies have focused on the discourse that students produce, some of these discussions have examined the broader issue of the role of composition theorists, scholars, and teachers in society and the degree to which they are capable of bringing about progressive social change through their own actions. In other words, some compositionists have begun to ask if we might become *public intellectuals,* and they have questioned whether or not there is anything particular about our discipline that might make us more viable candidates for this role than intellectuals working in other disciplines. In this chapter, I take up this discussion regarding compositionists as public intellectuals. I begin by examining the work of Stanley Fish, who suggests that public intellectualism is not possible in English studies (or any other discipline, for that matter). I draw upon the work of some of the social theorists that I have written about in chapters 3 and 4, and I apply their theories of the public to the current discussion of public intellectualism. By doing so, I hope to develop a more holistic, sophisticated analysis of the subject of public intellectualism in an effort to explain exactly how and to what degree compositionists might become more successful in their attempts to work toward a more democratic society. In the process, I describe a new approach to thinking about the roles that intellectuals might assume in their attempts to enact progressive political and social change.

STANLEY FISH, JÜRGEN HABERMAS, AND THE QUESTION OF THE PUBLIC INTELLECTUAL

Certainly, the urge to make what we do in English studies more culturally relevant is of concern to nearly all of the members of the discipline. In fact, the desire to influence public opinion and bring about progressive societal change is of interest to scholars and intellectuals in nearly every discipline. Many of us have begun to ask what we can do to help bring about changes in society through public forums. Scholarly journals and edited collections in English studies are filled with essays by authors who question whether or not intellectuals are capable of moving beyond disciplinary and academic borders to engage in deliberation and debate with larger public audiences. In English studies, scholars such as Michael Bèrubè, Cary Nelson, Bruce Robbins, and others have enabled us to reconsider our roles within English departments and to recognize the political functions of academic work and the ways that universities can serve as vehicles for activism. In composition, scholars including Ellen Cushman and Sidney

Dobrin have put forth interesting and important investigations of the particular role of compositionists in bringing about change in both the academy and in society as a whole. In short, the desire to become a public intellectual, one who speaks to diverse audiences on issues that affect segments of society outside of academia, has been discussed from a variety of perspectives, and some scholars have put forth some careful and constructive strategies for moving toward public intellectualism.

However, despite our inclinations, bringing about progressive societal change is not easy for intellectuals—or for anyone else for that matter. It is quite difficult to enter into public debate in nearly any form, and intellectuals are no better equipped to deal with the complex array of forces in the public sphere than are other members of society. As some scholars have noted, our jobs in the academy do not necessarily contain a democratic element, and to do those jobs effectively often leaves us with little time for activism outside of the academy. Stanley Fish, for example, suggests that academic work has little effect on public issues and opinions and that only those who have the frequent attention of vast segments of a society can be considered effective public intellectuals. In order to fully understand Fish's perspective on the question of the public intellectual, it is necessary first to understand how he defines the subject. In *Professional Correctness: Literary Studies and Political Change,* Fish offers the following definition:

> A public intellectual is someone who takes as his or her subject matters of public concern, and *has the public's attention.* Since one cannot gain that attention from the stage of the academy (except by some happy contingency) academics, by definition, are not candidates for the role of the public intellectual. Whatever the answer to the question "How does one get to be a public intellectual?" we know it won't be "by joining the academy." (118)

Based upon this definition, it is easy to see why he believes that public intellectualism is not available to most members of the academy. Certainly, we must agree with him that we cannot gain the attention of "the public" from the stage of the academy, and, if we accept this definition of public intellectualism, we must agree with Fish that it is not possible to assume this role while maintaining our positions in the academy. To be fair, Fish works from a long tradition that defines the public intellectual as someone who speaks to the masses on matters of general interest. In this respect, he is correct in suggesting that this sort of public intellectual does not exist in our society at present. Thinkers like Albert Einstein, who was seen as a sage on any number of intellectual issues, are few and far between today—particularly here in the United States. In the postmodern world, society no longer turns to intellectuals for guidance on broad social and political issues. However, what I'd like to suggest in the following pages is that even though public intellectuals in the traditional sense no longer exist (and perhaps rightly so), intellectuals who are interested in participating in social and political debates in society still have a number of options available to them. Effectively exercising these options requires that we go beyond the traditional sense of public intellectual work.

Interestingly, Fish's definition of a public intellectual seems to contain many of the same conceptions as another important thinker whom I've already discussed: Jürgen Habermas. In *The Structural Transformation of the Public Sphere,* as you will recall from chapters 3 and 4, Habermas offers an analysis of the bourgeois public sphere as a model for how forms of the public sphere might be formed in the present and future. Where Habermas examines the location of public discourse—labeled "the public sphere" by many theorists—Fish examines the degree to which modern-day intellectuals might enter and influence the discourse produced in this sphere. Both Habermas and Fish suggest that today it is very difficult to elicit democratic political and social change through public discourse. Habermas suggests that the public sphere eroded, and its erosion can be "clearly documented with regard to the transformation of the public sphere's preeminent institution, the press" (181). He concludes that the bourgeois public sphere disappeared with the emergence of "welfare-state mass democracy" (184). In other words, Habermas suggests that for citizens today, the public sphere no longer exists, and, consequently, public discourse does not exist in a form that might enable citizens to bring about progressive social change. While Fish does not examine the history of the bourgeois public sphere, he does suggest that for intellectuals there was a time when academics had the opportunity to engage in public discourse for the purpose of bringing about changes in society or at least swaying public opinion. He writes:

> As things stand now, the public does not look to academics for *general* wisdom, in part because (as is often complained) academics are not trained to speak on everything, only on particular things, but more importantly because academics do not have a stage or pulpit from which their pronouncements, should they be so inclined to make them, could be broadcast . . . I say "as things stand now" because academics, or at least a visible number of them, once did have such a pulpit, the college president or major deanship, offices that for a long time carried with them not only the possibility but the obligation of addressing issues of public concern. (119–20)

Clearly, both Habermas and Fish look to the past, seeing a time when an arena for public discourse (be it a sphere or a pulpit) did indeed exist. Despite the fact that they differ on their conceptions of how these arenas disappeared, both suggest that the true public sphere in the sense that they write of does not exist in society today.

In addition, both Habermas and Fish share a number of other conceptions regarding the location and activity of public discourse. Both, for example, suggest that public discourse is only worthwhile if it reaches a large segment of the population who are able to act upon it in some way. Furthermore, they both seem to suggest that public discourse must address an eclectic audience, since speaking to an assorted constituency is the only way to bring about widespread changes in thinking and practice. In other words, they assume that public discourse must address the "general public," and the term public is often taken to encompass all members of a society, or at least a representative microcosm of them.

As I've mentioned earlier, Habermas's account of the public sphere stresses the singularity of the bourgeois conception of the public sphere, its claim to be *the* public arena, in the singular. Habermas asserts that the bourgeoisie in seventeenth- and eighteenth-century Europe conceived of "the public sphere as something properly theirs" (24). His narrative seems to agree with this conception, since it "casts the emergence of additional publics as a late development signaling fragmentation and decline" (Fraser 122). That is, Habermas seems to suggest that any departure from this conception of a singular public sphere is a departure from the ideal. Habermas's narrative is based upon an underlying assumption: that confining public discourse to a single, over-arching public sphere is a desirable and positive move, whereas the proliferation of discourse in a multiplicity of public spaces represents a departure from, rather than an advance toward, democracy.

In similar fashion, Fish seems to argue that public discourse must always address a single public consisting of all or many members in a society. He asks the question, "What do we say to the *public,* that generalized body that wants, not unreasonably, to believe that the cultural activities it sustains have a benign relationship to its concerns and values" (115–16). There are several aspects of this question that parallel Habermas's conception of the public sphere. First, Fish asks "What do we say to 'the *public,*'" a question that seems to suggest that there is just one singular group of individuals to whom intellectuals might speak. Moreover, he emphasizes this point by referring to the public as a "generalized body"—a definition that seems to exclude the sort of subaltern or counterpublics that Negt, Kluge, and Fraser discuss. Finally, Fish suggests that the topics of public discourse must be confined to matters of common concern, since he appears to be most mindful of the publics' "concerns and values." Fish reinforces this belief that public discourse must be of common concern when he argues that the public intellectual is "someone to whom the public regularly looks for illumination on any number of (indeed all) issues" and makes his point even clearer when he suggests that the public does not look to academics for this *general* wisdom" (119).

Quite simply, Habermas and Fish suggest that the only discourse truly worthy of being called *public* discourse (and similarly, the only intellectual worthy of being called a public intellectual) is that which addresses a large segment of society comprised of a diverse cross-section of the general population and speaks about matters that are of concern to all or most of these assorted individuals. While all of these conceptions hold true in the traditional sense, I'd like to suggest some ways that we can move beyond the traditional sense of what it means to be a public intellectual. In fact, I would argue that it is necessary for us to rethink what it means to be an intellectual working in the public sphere today, and this rethinking requires us to take into account the particularities of the postmodern world in which we live and work. We can, and should, move beyond the longstanding conventional definition of public intellectualism if we are to influence public decision-making and action in society today.

RETHINKING PUBLIC INTELLECTUALISM

At this point, I'd like to return to several of the most significant points that Nancy Fraser makes concerning the public sphere. Fraser, as you will recall, questions many of the assumptions that Habermas makes in *The Structural Transformation,* and, to my thinking, offers a more critical and useful stance on the role citizens might play in public spheres. In "Rethinking the Public Sphere," she makes several suggestions toward a new conception of discourse in public spheres, suggestions that I've applied to the discussion of public writing. Interestingly, many of these same suggestions apply to the role of intellectuals in public spheres. While I'm not proposing that all of Fraser's suggestions refute what Fish has to say, I am proposing that much of Fraser's work is pertinent and applicable to the question of the public intellectual.

There are a number of suggestions that Fraser makes regarding public spheres that can be useful in rethinking how intellectuals might have greater political and social import. For example, her analysis of the sites in which public discourse (and by extension, public intellectualism) can occur is quite compelling. Counter to both Habermas's and Fish's confidence in an all-encompassing site for public discourse that is comprised of a cross-section of society, Fraser contends that in stratified societies, "arrangements that accommodate contestation among a plurality of competing publics better promote the ideal of participatory parity than does a single, comprehensive, overarching public" (122). As I have explained earlier, she suggests that in societies whose basic structure generates unequal social groups in relations of dominance and subordination (as is the case in the United States), full parity of participation in public discourse is not feasible. Despite the fact that all members of a society may be *allowed* to participate in public discourse, it is impossible to insulate special discursive arenas from the effects of societal inequality. This being the case, she goes on to assert that the disadvantages that certain groups face are only exacerbated where there is only one single arena for public discourse. If there were only one site for public discourse, members of subordinate groups would have no arenas for deliberation among themselves about their needs, objectives, and strategies. They would have no "venues in which to undertake communicative processes that were not, as it were, under the supervision of dominant groups" (123). In other words, if there were only a single public sphere, subaltern groups would have no discursive spaces in which to deliberate free of oppression.

While I'm not suggesting that intellectuals are marginalized per se, I do think that in many circumstances, they speak from and for marginalized viewpoints. In our investigations of the critical categories of race, class, and gender, we have examined the ways that certain groups have been excluded from various features of dominant society, and much of our public discourse would and does address these inequalities. Radical scholars and teachers in composition are among those who are most interested in moving beyond academic discourse and participating more fully in social and political debates as public intellectuals. I think it's fair to say that the perspectives of these scholars and teachers are often excluded from the larger public discussions in, for example, the media.

Fraser suggests that it is advantageous for subordinated groups to constitute alternative sites of public discourse—what she calls subaltern counterpublics. She envisions these sites as "parallel discursive arenas where members of subordinated social groups invent and circulate counterdiscourses to formulate oppositional interpretations of their identities, interests, and needs" (123). Fraser sites for example the late twentieth-century U.S. feminist subaltern counterpublic, with its diverse array of journals, bookstores, publishing companies, film and video distribution networks, lecture series, research centers, academic programs, conferences, conventions, festivals, and local meeting places (123). While subaltern counterpublics are not always inherently democratic or progressive, they do emerge in response to exclusions and omissions within dominant publics, and as such they help expand discursive space. In general, the proliferation of subaltern counterpublics means a widening of discursive contestation, and "that is a good thing in stratified societies" (124). Subaltern counterpublics can serve at least two functions. On the one hand, they function as spaces where oppressed others can withdraw, regroup, and heal; and on the other hand, they function as "training grounds" and bases for the development of discourse or action that might agitate or disrupt wider publics.

Intellectuals can take part in creating such counterpublics, and must also look for alternative sites in which to voice their opinions on social and political issues. Obviously, public discourse need not be limited to a single discursive arena that reaches a huge cross-section of society. What I'd like to suggest is that we look to the variety of spaces already available to us for work as activist intellectuals. For example, we can promote change in our communities and public spheres through three general and interconnected means: through the classroom, through scholarship, and through our own public actions. These means must reinforce each other if our activism is to have any effect at all. Additionally, we must not make the mistake of assuming that our individual work will bring about sweeping changes in the thoughts or actions of society or the public as a whole. Even our use of the term "public" is problematic, as the public is a space filled with contradictory voices, varying opinions, and separate discourses in an endless number of combinations. But what is important to note is that our work can dramatically affect the individual lives of those we come into contact with and can have valuable and significant effects in our communities in general—as long as we do not assume that these changes will occur overnight or that they will necessarily affect society as a whole.

We might resist looking at social change on the macro level, for in doing this we will come to feel that social and political forces are unalterable in the present, and we will soon agree with Fish in saying that a time when academics are capable of making social change "is not coming soon, and I do not feel that anything you or I could do will bring it closer" (2). Instead, we might begin to view social change on the micro level of interaction and allow it to fit into our immediate situations and communities. We might begin to conceive of ourselves as activist intellectuals, individuals who work through, around, and beside our academic occupations to bring about social reform on local levels. The situation for the intellectual who wishes to have some social agency is not black and white; we can choose to work with the smaller communities and individuals we come into contact with in our everyday lives. Rather than looking for immediate, widespread results that we ourselves have brought about individually, we might strive for cumulative change brought about by many individuals over extended periods of time. Couldn't we reconceive of our roles as teacher-scholars to include a wider range of possibilities, both in terms of what we hope to be and what we'd like to accomplish? We are capable of various forms of public intellectualism— but only if we can realize this goal *through* our intellectual occupations, not instead of them. It is possible, as Richard Ohmann suggests, to "work where you are and will be to challenge entrenched inequality and the arrogance of power that nearly satu-rate our main arenas of public discourse and social action" (256).

Fraser also critiques the assumption, which both Habermas and Fish seem to share, that discourse in public spheres should be limited to deliberation about the common good, and that the appearance of private issues and interests is always undesirable. What Habermas and Fish both seem to argue is that public spheres must be sites where private persons deliberate about "public matters." In a sense, they are correct that matters of public debate must affect a number of individuals to be of importance to society as a whole. However, what they fail to recognize is that the term "public" is ambiguous and open to interpretation. Fraser argues that there are several usages of the term "public," and in regard to the sense that the term might mean "of concern to everyone," she suggests that only participants can decide what is of common con-cern, and there is no guarantee that all of them will agree. Fraser suggests that the term "public" is "ambiguous between what objectively affects or has an impact on everyone as seen from an outsider's perspective, and what is recognized as a matter of common concern by participants" (128–29). Only participants can decide what is of common concern to them. However, there is no guarantee that they will all agree, and what will actually count as a matter of common concern will be decided through discursive contestation. Any consensus that has been reached through such contesta-tion will have been reached "through deliberative processes tainted by the effects of dominance and subordination" (131). In other words, those who are in power get to decide what is a public issue and what is not.

Fraser asserts that the terms "public" and "private" are not simply absolute defini-tions of the two basic spheres in society; they are "cultural classifications and rhetori-cal labels" (131). As such, they work ideologically to reinforce the boundaries of pub-lic discourse in ways that disadvantage subordinate groups and individuals. For example, as I've mentioned in earlier chapters, the issue of domestic violence was, until quite recently, considered to be a private matter between what was assumed to be a fairly small number of heterosexual couples. Feminists were in the minority in think-ing that "domestic violence against women was a matter of common concern and thus a legitimate topic of public discourse" (129). The feminist counterpublic, however, helped to develop and spread a new conception of domestic violence as a widespread systemic feature of male-dominated societies. Only through their sustained debate and negotiation with other spheres, both public and private, were feminists able to make domestic violence a matter that was seen as a legitimate common concern.

While Fish suggests that a public intellectual must "take as his or her subject mat-ters of public concern," I would argue that these concerns need not address matters of interest to all or most of the members in a society. Instead, activist intellectuals might take up matters that address particular groups and their interests. Fish notes a number of intellectuals who take up more specialized causes, but he suggests that they are not able to speak on more than one specific issue and are not, therefore, public intellectuals. He writes:

> These [rent for a day intellectuals] and others will only get the call when the particular issue with which they are identified takes centre-stage and should that issue lose its sexiness, their media careers will be over. That is why they are "cameo" intellectuals or intellectuals for a day; a public intellectual, on the other hand, is the *public's* intellectual; that is, he or she is someone to whom the public regularly looks for illumination on any number of (indeed all) issues, and, as things stand now, the public does not look to academics for this *general* wisdom, in part because (as is often complained) academics are not trained to speak on everything, only on particular things. (119)

I would argue that our definition of the activist intellectual need not be confined to those who can speak about all issues to all people. Instead, we should view activist intellectuals as those who can speak to *any* group outside of the academy on any issues—particular or general. There is nothing wrong with taking up specific issues in public debates, and our professional and personal interests often lead us to these issues.

Fraser also questions the assumption that it is possible for interlocutors in any public debate to actually bracket status differentials and to participate in discourse as if all of the members of a public sphere were social equals. Fraser suggests that in any public sphere, it is impossible to effectively bracket social differences among interlocutors. She writes:

> But were they [the differences between interlocutors] really effectively bracketed? The revisionist historiography suggests that they were not. Rather, discursive interaction within the bourgeois public sphere was governed by protocols of style and decorum that were themselves correlates and markers of status inequality. These functioned informally to marginalize women and members of the plebeian classes and to prevent them from participating as peers. (119)

In this respect, Fraser is talking about informal impediments to participatory parity that can persist even after everyone is formally and legally licensed to participate. Certainly, there are no legal restrictions on intellectuals participating in public debates in the United States today, regardless of the circumstances. Intellectuals are free to speak on practically any topic in society today, and, as Fish notes, he himself has seen a number of them "peering out from [his] television screen" (118). While there are no legal barriers keeping intellectuals from entering public discourse, there are other more subtle forces that cannot be easily disposed of through legislation. Fraser notes a number of these informal impediments that might keep citizens in general, and intellectuals in particular, from participating in public discourse. She cites, for example, a familiar contemporary example drawn from feminist research. It has been documented that in mixed-sex deliberations, men tend to interrupt women more than women interrupt men; men also tend to speak more than women; and women's interventions are more often ignored or not responded to than men's. Deliberation and the appearance of participatory parity can serve as a mask for domination. Acknowledging the work of theorists like Jane Mansbridge, Fraser argues that various manipulations of discourse are often used to cloak nearly imperceptible modes of control. Fraser argues that

> the transformation of "I" into "we" brought about through political deliberation can easily mask subtle forms of control. Even the language people use as they reason together usually favors one way of seeing things and discourages others. Subordinate groups sometimes cannot find the right voice or words to express their thoughts, and when they do, they discover they are not heard. [They] are silenced, encouraged to keep their wants inchoate, and heard to say "yes" when what they have said is "no." (119)

Many of these feminist insights into ways in which discourse is used to mask domination and imbalances of power can be applied to other kinds of unequal relations, like those based on class or ethnicity. They alert us to the ways in which "social inequalities can infect deliberation, even in the absence of any formal exclusions" (119). In this respect, the bracketing of differences and social inequalities in public discourse cannot actually be enacted, and making the assumption that such bracketing can be enacted actually works to the advantage of dominant groups in a public sphere and to the disadvantage of subordinates. In most cases, it would be more appropriate to *unbracket* these inequalities by foregrounding and thematizing them. Doing this would help to eliminate some of the more pernicious uses of discourse in public deliberation. The assumption that public discourse occurs in arenas that can overlook, bracket, or disregard social and cultural differences is counterfactual.

   Undoubtedly, these inequalities taint the deliberation of intellectuals who engage in various forms of public discourse, and the effects of these inequalities are certainly obstacles that intellectuals must recognize and negotiate if they are to deliberate successfully in public settings. The ideology of gender, like the ideologies of race and class, constructs and reconstructs all sorts of discursive interaction. The imbalances of power that exist in nearly every aspect of society are not likely to magically disappear when some or even all of the actors involved are degreed academics. But the awareness of these imbalances is one step toward overcoming them. Compositionists, in particular, seem well-suited to recognize and surmount some of the effects of this inequality. Much of our scholarship in recent years has examined the role of ideology in shaping conversations, and our particular rhetorical awareness might help us to foreground situations wherein public discourse is being affected by particular social forces. Compositionists should be quick to recognize that social differences shape public discourse in significant ways. We also need to continue efforts to establish new theories of public discourse that acknowledge differences in thinking and writing—theories that might make us more astute as activist intellectuals.

Public Teachers

If we accept that activist intellectualism might consist of more than addressing a singular, overarching public sphere, and that our discourse need not be confined to matters of "common concern," we might be able to conceive of a new definition of what it means to be an activist intellectual. Rather than supposing that our activist efforts must occur in just one way, we might begin to see a variety of opportunities for work that influences political and social decision making and action in society. Our work in the classroom, for example, might be seen as perhaps the most important and effective avenue of political and social change that is available to us. It's unfortunate that some of us involved in the production of knowledge in English studies seem to feel that our work is somehow divorced from the lives, actions, and issues outside of our universities. While recent theories and pedagogies in both literature and composition have powerfully changed how we teach, we have largely "failed to make a convincing case beyond the classroom for the new view[s] of literacy that we profess inside it" (Harris, "Research, Teaching, Public Argument" 324). Our classroom work *must*, then, attempt to help students develop the real skills that they will need to be successful in their lives both inside and outside of the university. By "skills" I mean not only how to write effectively for their future classes and careers (although this is certainly important), but also how to make well-informed decisions about the political and social issues that affect them. English departments, and compositionists in particular, play a unique and powerful role in the modern university. At nearly all colleges and universities, students are required to complete at least one and usually two semesters of first-year English. What is most significant, as Evan Watkins notes in *Work Time: English Departments and the Circulation of Cultural Value,* is "the appropriateness of the gatekeeper image to the position of English departments, not only in community colleges but throughout the educational system" (5). In reality, *everyone* who earns an undergraduate degree in the United States has spent at least one year in frequent contact with an English instructor or professor. First-year English is, after all, something close to a rite of passage into the educated middle class. If we aim collectively to give our students, as Robert Scholes urges, "the kind of knowledge and skill that will enable them to make sense of their worlds, to determine their interests, both individual and collective, to see through the manipulations of all sorts of texts in all sorts of media, and to express themselves in some appropriate manner" (15), doesn't it stand to reason that we would certainly, albeit indirectly, bring about a greater awareness in the public of social and political forces? And isn't awareness a necessary and important first step?

But as I mentioned, we cannot count on collective efforts or larger changes in society. We can only hope to enable the fifty or more students we come into contact with at least once a week to become more critical of the world around them. And we cannot expect to make changes in more than a few of their lives each semester. Once again, we need to avoid looking for sweeping changes and monumental efforts toward societal engagement. But what we must not overlook is the individual lives that we stand a very good chance of affecting in our classrooms. As teachers, intellectuals "train critical readers and writers and prepare those who will move into positions of power and authority throughout society" (Merod 39). We might look to our role in the classroom as a trickle-down effect. If we are able to empower just a few students each year to "read" their own lives, develop their own opinions, and respond in meaningful ways, we will have affected a considerable number of individuals during the course of our careers. And these same students will soon become members, by and large, of the educated middle class—members who are very likely to influence the actions and opinions of others. And, while we cannot quantify how effective our efforts might be, it doesn't seem too optimistic to assume that they will be palpable.

While classroom assignments that superficially attempt to engage students in public debates—such as current-events essays, letters to the editor, taking-a-stand papers, and the like—can "quickly seem absurdly decontextualized and formulaic in classrooms that are cut off from meaningful contact with the real public discourse of society" (Harris, "Research, Teaching" 324), a thorough and concrete approach to public writing (based upon the criteria I've outlined in chap. 4) can substantially change the ways students read public texts and respond with their own. This kind of work helps students develop a critical self-awareness of their relation to the public world, and I would like to believe, as does Patricia Bizzell, that "such development leads in progressive directions" ("Patricia Bizzell's Statement" par. 5).

Public Scholars

While many scholars might agree that our classrooms are viable sites for encountering and producing public texts, fewer would agree that scholarship in composition studies is also a tenable space through which we can practice activism. Some argue that we are what we are only through clearly defined and rigidly structured modes of discourse, and to say things in ways unrelated to these particular modes is to risk losing our professional identities. But as scholars of discourse, our work can both be true to existing definitions of what it is we do and also move outside of our own discipline. In recent years, for example, many compositionists have begun to concentrate on the internal rhetoric of discourse communities. All discourse communities have their own specialized means of producing and circulating knowledge, and these discourse communities use these specifically to represent and describe their particular outlook on the world. Analyzing these discourse communities "substantiates and extends the study of general rhetoric, which has been concerned with the specialized languages of discourse communities only as they enter into the shared space of public debate" (Killingsworth 7). Scholars in composition who are interested in questions of public writing, rhetoric, and social activism might begin their scholarly work with studies of the various discourse communities that come into contact with each other through various public spaces. This places discourse specialists in a unique position within the academy both to "do what we do" and to extend our work to investigate intersections with other modes of discourse at the same time. Thus, we would reinforce our own disciplinary foundations through the study of other disciplines and discourse communities and how they circulate knowledge.

As the various discourse communities define themselves by their individual discourses, one result is that they often find themselves unable to communicate effectively with each other and often have difficulty entering the loosely agreed upon language of public debate. Specialists—whether they be academics, politicians, or members of other specialized discourse communities—are often unable to create strong communicative links with public groups, "links that would support a strong power base for reformative actions" (Killingsworth 7). As discourse specialists, it should be our goal to create such links between discourse communities. This work might begin by devoting more attention to the issues that affect communities outside of our own and how they are resolved or perpetuated through discourse. Much of the recent work in English has begun to do this through cultural studies, gender studies, and other interdisciplinary investigations. By exploring the intersections of different discourse communities in public spaces, we might discover ways to build communicative links between different groups and individuals.

If we begin to explore other discourse communities through our own scholarship, we might develop a greater awareness of how these various discourses come together in public spaces, how our own specialized type of discourse might benefit from exposure to the other types of discourse that we might encounter; and, ultimately, we might discover how we can best deliver our own specialized knowledge into contact with others in various public arenas. A critical examination of competing academic discourses is an important topic for compositionists. Understanding how academics interact among themselves through their scholarly journals and how they relate to different or competing discourses in public spaces might begin to teach us how we can best deliver our own messages to these groups. By understanding their language, we might gain the ability to speak to them in ways with which they are familiar. Much of the intractability of modern social problems is due to the inability of concerned discourse communities to construct working relationship through language for the purpose of cooperative social action. Resolution and action are nearly impossible when different discourse communities are unable to communicate effectively. Careful studies of how different discourse communities generate and distribute knowledge might begin to give us the exigency we need to talk to a larger audience than "a few of our friends'" (Fish, *Professional Correctness* 1). Through our scholarship, we might begin to build bridges between our own work and that of other communities—all of which might begin to enable social change.

Public Workers

Our private efforts are necessary in bringing about public change through writing and physical work. Some of the most influential and important intellectuals involved in the study of discourse have recognized the value and importance of active work outside of the academy. Noam Chomsky, for example, has long been active in social and political debates. In an interview with Gary A. Olson and Lester Faigley, Chomsky comments on his work in linguistics and his political work outside of academe, stating that he has "two full-time professional careers, each of them quite demanding" ("Language, Politics, and Composition" 64). Chomsky even suggests that his social and political work is more culturally relevant than his work in linguistics, as he sees himself first "as a *human being,* and your time as a *human being* should be socially useful" (65). Paulo Freire was also noted for his work through both educational structures and through active political involvement. In a different interview with Olson, Freire asserted that "a progressive teacher, a progressive thinker, a progressive politician many times has his or her left foot inside the system, the structures, and the right foot out of it" ("History, *Praxis,* and Change" 163). Likewise, in an interview shortly before his death, Michel

Foucault emphasizes his urge to make social changes by "working inside the body of society . . . participating in this enterprise without delegating the responsibility to any specialist" (160). Our work outside the academy is vitally important; we cannot assume that attention to social and political debates inside of the academy is sufficient. While opportunities for social activism might not be as open to most of us as they have been for the intellectuals just mentioned, opportunities are nonetheless available. We might join organizations in our neighborhoods and communities. We could give a few hours each month to causes we believe in. While some would argue that academics are too busy fulfilling the work requirements necessary to earn tenure and gain promotions, we might take an example from Chomsky, Freire, and others—all of whom found time for social work in addition to active and productive careers.

Also, we bring our own lives into our scholarship and teaching. What we do as individuals in our private lives informs what we do as members of academia; productive intellectual work depends on our ability to import real issues into the work we do in our classrooms and that which enters conversations in our scholarly journals. Active work in public spaces translates directly into more dynamic and engaged scholarship and teaching.

Through these three interconnected means of engagement with public issues— through the classroom, through scholarship, and through our lives outside of academia— we might arrive at a new definition of activist intellectualism, one that takes into account the smaller roles and opportunities that are more readily available to us than the narrow definition of reaching vast audiences in short periods of time. We might begin to extend our definitions of activist intellectualism to accommodate the variety of opportunities we have to foster cooperative public connections. No one of these means is sufficient in and of itself, nor will we be able to bring about sweeping changes individually or immediately. But if we begin to refigure our roles as socially active intellectuals and understand that opportunities for activism are open to all of us, we can begin to have significant social and political effects. We need, as Ellen Cushman notes in *The Rhetorician as an Agent of Social Change,* "a deeper consideration of the civic purpose of our *positions* in the academy, of what we do with our knowledge, for whom, and by what means" (12). Activist intellectuals might be then, quite simply, members of academe who take steps to bring more voices, more discourse, and a greater degree of communication to public debates, and in turn bring about social change.

CONCLUSIONS—OR NEW BEGINNINGS

In this work, I've tried to put forth a careful and thorough examination of what may very well become the next significant keyword in composition studies: *public*. As more and more compositionists investigate various aspects of this term and devise new ways of extending their research, scholarship, and teaching to more fully inquire into the concept of "publicness," I am sure that the discipline will give birth to new discussions, publications, and applications of this concept. It is my hope that this work is useful in promoting new approaches to the concept of the public and its usefulness to the work we do as scholars and teachers of writing. I hope that this discussion will extend current and future theoretical investigations in ways that allow us to understand exactly what public discourse might entail. In addition, I hope that writing instructors find this material useful as they attempt to facilitate students' writing in public spheres.

As you will recall, I began this project with an examination of the recent history of the discipline of composition studies. Over the past few years, I've come to realize that many of the conversations in our discipline build upon the preceding work in the field in attempts to more fully and accurately define and explain how and why writing is produced. Since its emergence as an academic discipline in the 1960s, composition gradually expanded its focus from the individual writer, to social notions of how knowledge is produced, to more political investigations of discourse. I see the recent interest in public writing, public discourse, and public intellectualism as a continuation of that very expansion. More and more scholars in composition studies are interested in moving beyond academic discourse, in both the classroom and scholarship, and toward uses of discourse that might have more significance in shaping the world that we live in.

Like much of the research in composition studies, this project began as an investigation into a subject that is, to us, fairly new. Explicit conversations on public writing and public intellectualism have only emerged in our discipline in the last half-decade of the twentieth century. While compositionists have been interested in making student writing (as well as their own writing) more socially useful, at least since the early 1970s, it is only recently that scholars have made use of the term *public* in published articles and book chapters.

While I hope that this work contains something of merit for the scholar or teacher who reads it, something that they could not have found in any other source, I am, of course, indebted to much of the work that precedes this one. Particularly useful to me was Susan Wells's "Rogue Cops and Health Care: What Do We Want from Public Writing?" Her suggestion that writing teachers need to build, or take part in building, discursive domains where student writing takes a public role was a call-to-arms for me, and I hope that this book in some way takes part in building new discursive domains, whether they be theoretical or pedagogical.

In addition, Wells's essay introduced me to social theorists like Richard Sennett, Jürgen Habermas, Oskar Negt, Alexander Kluge, and most notably, Nancy Fraser. I quickly discovered that while overt investigations of the public sphere are somewhat new to composition studies, there is a long history of discussions and publications on the subject in philosophy and in the political and social sciences. Like many scholars in composition studies over the past thirty or so years, I found it astoundingly fruitful to incorporate discussions from other fields into our own conversations. In fact, this project would not exist in its present form were it not for the work of these theorists who are, at least in terms of their disciplinary affiliations, outside of composition studies.

I hope that I have shown that our recent investigations into publicness, investigations that we have undertaken as teachers, theorists, scholars, intellectuals, and citizens, emerge from a long history of research and scholarship that inquires into how our work as compositionists might be most productive. Placing this most recent move in its historical context might better allow us to extend it in more meaningful directions in the future. I believe that the incorporation of the work of the social theorists that I've addressed might be useful to further discussions of public writing and public intellectualism in composition studies. I have found the work of the many scholars in composition who have written about public writing and public intellectualism to be rewarding in terms of my own teaching practices, and I hope that this study is equally rewarding for others in the future.

WORKS CITED
INDEX

WORKS CITED

Adler-Kassner, Linda, Robert Crooks, and Ann Waters, eds. *Writing the Community: Concepts and Models for Service-Learning.* Urbana: NCTE, 1997.

Anderson, Worth, Cynthia Best, Alycia Black, John Hurst, Brandt Miller, and Susan Miller. "Cross-Curricular Underlife: A Collaborative Report on Ways with Academic Words." *College Composition and Communication* 41 (1990): 11–36.

Arendt, Hannah. *The Human Condition.* Chicago: U of Chicago P, 1958.

Aronowitz, Stanley. "Is a Democracy Possible? The Decline of the Public in the American Debate." Robbins, *Phantom Public Sphere* 75–92.

Aronowitz, Stanley, and Henry Giroux. *Postmodern Education: Politics, Culture, and Social Criticism.* Minneapolis: U of Minnesota P, 1991.

Ashton-Jones, Evelyn. "Conversation, Collaboration, and the Politics of Gender." *Feminine Principles and Women's Experience in American Composition and Rhetoric.* Ed. Janet Emig and Louise Phelps. Pittsburgh: U of Pittsburgh P, 1995. 5–26.

Auerbach, Erich. *Scenes from the Drama of European Literature.* New York: Meridian, 1959.

Berlin, James A. *Cultural Studies in the English Classroom.* Portsmouth, NH: Boynton, 1992.

———. "Rhetoric and Ideology in the Writing Class." *College English* 50 (1988): 477–94.

———. *Rhetoric and Reality: Writing Instruction in American Colleges, 1900–1985.* Carbondale: Southern Illinois UP, 1987.

———. *Rhetorics, Poetics, and Cultures: Refiguring College English Studies.* Urbana: NCTE, 1996.

Bizzell, Patricia A. *Academic Discourse and Critical Consciousness.* Pittsburgh: U of Pittsburgh P, 1992.

———. "Patricia Bizzell's Statement." *Teaching Writing for Social Change.* 11 Aug. 1999 <http://www.hu.mtu.edu/cccc/98/social/bizzell.htm>.

Britton, James. *Language and Learning.* Harmondsworth: Penguin, 1970.

Brodkey, Linda. "On the Subjects of Class and Gender in 'The Literacy Letters.'" *College English* 51 (1989): 125–41.

———. "Writing on the Bias." *College English* 56 (1994): 527–47.

Bruffee, Kenneth A. "Collaborative Writing and 'The Conversation of Mankind.'" *College English* 46 (1984): 635–52.

———. "Social Construction, Language, and the Authority of Knowledge: A Bibliographical Essay." *College English* 48 (1986): 773–89.

———. "The Way Out: A Critical Survey of Innovations in College Teaching, with Special Reference to the December 1971 Issue of *CE.*" *College English* 33 (1972): 457–70.

Calhoun, Craig, ed. *Habermas and the Public Sphere.* Cambridge: MIT P, 1992.

Carson, Rachel. *Silent Spring.* New York: Houghton, 1962.

Chapman, David, Jeanette Harns, and Christine Hult. "Agents for Change: Undergraduate Writing Programs in Departments of English." *Rhetoric Review* 13 (1995): 421–35.

Chomsky, Noam. *Syntactic Structures*. New York: Peter Lang, 1975.

Christensen, Francis. "A Generative Rhetoric of the Paragraph." *College Composition and Communication* 14 (1963): 155–61.

Clifford, John, and John Schlib, eds. *Writing Theory and Critical Theory*. New York: MLA, 1994.

Cooper, Marilyn M., and Michael Holzman. *Writing as Social Action*. Portsmouth, NH: Boynton, 1989.

Crowley, Sharon. "Composition's Ethic of Service, the Universal Requirement, and the Discourse of Student Need." *JAC* 15 (1995): 227–40.

Cushman, Ellen. "Opinion: The Public Intellectual." *College English* 61 (1999): 328–37.

———. "The Rhetorician as an Agent of Social Change." *College Composition and Communication* 47 (1996): 7–28.

Deemer, Charles. "English Composition as a Happening." *College English* 29 (1967): 121–26.

Dixon, John. *Growth Through English (Set in the Perspective of the Seventies)*. 3rd ed. London: NATE, 1967.

Dobrin, Sidney I. "English Departments and the Question of Disciplinarity." *College English* 59 (1997): 692–99.

———. "Race and the Public Intellectual: A Conversation with Michael Eric Dyson." *JAC* 17 (1997): 143–82.

Drew, Julie. "Cultural Composition: Stuart Hall on Ethnicity and the Discursive Turn." *JAC* 18 (1998): 171–96.

Elbow, Peter. *Writing Without Teachers*. New York: Oxford UP, 1973.

Emig, Janet. *The Composing Process of Twelfth Graders*. Research Report No. 13. Urbana: NCTE, 1971.

Faigley, Lester. *Fragments of Rationality: Postmodernity and the Subject of Composition*. Pittsburgh: U of Pittsburgh P, 1992.

Fish, Stanley. *Is There a Text in This Class? The Authority of Interpretive Communities*. Cambridge: Harvard UP, 1980.

———. *Professional Correctness: Literary Studies and Political Change*. Oxford: Clarendon P, 1995.

Fishman, Stephen M., and Lucille Parkinson McCarthy. "Teaching for Student Change: A Deweyan Alternative to Radical Pedagogy." *College Composition and Communication* 47 (1996): 343–66.

Fitts, Karen, and Alan France, eds. *Left Margins: Cultural Studies and Composition Pedagogy*. Albany: State U of New York P, 1995.

Flower, Linda S., and John R. Hayes. "A Cognitive Process Theory of Writing." *College Composition and Communication* 32 (1981): 365–87.

Foucault, Michel. *Remarks on Marx: Conversations with Duccio Trombadori*. Trans. R. James Goldstein and James Casciato. New York: Semiotext(e), 1991.

Fraser, Nancy. "Politics, Culture, and the Public Sphere: Toward a Postmodern Conception." *Social Postmodernism: Beyond Identity Politics*. Ed. Linda L. Nicholson and Steven Seidman. Cambridge UP, 1995. 173–81.

———. "Rethinking the Public Sphere: A Contribution to the Critique of Actually Existing Democracy." *Habermas and the Public Sphere*. Ed. Craig Calhoun. Cambridge: MIT P, 1996. 109–42.

———. *Unruly Practices: Power, Discourse, and Gender in Contemporary Social Theory.* Minneapolis: U of Minnesota P, 1989.

Freire, Paulo. *Education for Critical Consciousness.* Trans. Myra Bergman Ramos. New York: Seabury, 1973.

———. *Pedagogy of the Oppressed.* Trans. Myra Bergman Ramos. New York: Continuum, 1970.

Fromm, Harold. "The Rhetoric and Politics of Environmentalism." *College English* 59 (1997): 946–50.

Gale, Xin Liu. *Teachers, Discourses, and Authority in the Postmodern Composition Classroom.* Albany: State U of New York P, 1996.

Gere, Anne Ruggles. "The Extracurriculum of Composition." *College Composition and Communication* 45 (1994): 75–92.

———. *Into the Field: Sites of Composition Studies.* New York: MLA, 1993.

Giroux, Henry A. *Postmodernism, Feminism, and Cultural Politics: Redrawing Educational Boundaries.* Albany: State U of New York P, 1991.

———. "Where Have All the Public Intellectuals Gone? Racial Politics, Pedagogy, and Disposable Youth." *JAC* 17 (1997): 191–206.

Goleman, Judith. *Working Theory.* Westport, CT: Bergin, 1995.

Gore, Al. Introduction. *Silent Spring.* By Rachel Carson. New York: Houghton, 1994. xv–xxvi.

Graff, Gerald. *Beyond the Culture Wars: How Teaching the Conflicts Can Revitalize American Education.* New York: Norton, 1993.

Habermas, Jürgen. *Communication and the Evolution of Society.* Trans. Thomas McCarthy. Boston: Beacon, 1979.

———. *Legitimation Crisis.* Trans. Thomas McCarthy. Boston: Beacon, 1981.

———. "The Public Sphere." *New German Critique* 3 (1974): 45–55.

———. *The Structural Transformation of the Public Sphere: An Inquiry into a Category Bourgeois Society.* Trans. Thomas Burger. Cambridge: MIT P, 1989.

———. *The Theory of Communicative Action: Lifeworld and System: A Critique of Functionalist Reason.* Trans. Thomas McCarthy. Boston: Beacon P, 1987.

———. *The Theory of Communicative Action: Reason and the Rationalization of Society.* Trans. Thomas McCarthy. Boston: Beacon P, 1984.

Hairston, Maxine. "The Winds of Change: Thomas Kuhn and the Revolution in the Teaching of Writing." *College Composition and Communication* 14 (1982): 14–26.

Halloran, S. Michael. "Rhetoric in the American College Curriculum: The Decline of Public Discourse." *Pre/Text* 3 (1982): 245–69.

Hansen, Miriam. Foreword. *The Public Sphere and Experience.* By Oskar Negt and Alexander Kluge. Minneapolis: U of Minnesota P, 1993. xxix–xlvii.

———. "Unstable Mixtures, Dilated Spheres: Negt and Kluge's *The Public Sphere and Experience.*" *Public Culture* 5 (1993): 179–212.

Harris, Joseph. "Negotiating the Contact Zone." *Journal of Basic Writing* 14 (1995): 27–42.

———. "The Other Reader." *JAC* 12 (1992) 121–38.

———. "Research, Teaching, Public Argument." *College Composition and Communication* 47 (1996): 323–24.

———. *A Teaching Subject: Composition since 1966.* Upper Saddle River: Prentice Hall, 1997.

Heilker, Paul. "Rhetoric Made Real: Civic Discourse and Writing Beyond the Curriculum." *Writing the Community: Concepts and Models for Service-Learning.* Ed. Linda Adler-Kassner, Robert Crooks, and Ann Waters. Urbana: NCTE, 1997. 71–78.

Held, David. *Introduction to Critical Theory: Horkheimer to Habermas.* Berkeley: U of California P, 1981.

Herndl, Carl G., and Stuart C. Brown. *Green Culture: Environmental Rhetoric in Contemporary America.* Madison: U of Wisconsin P, 1996.

Herzberg, Bruce. "Community Service and Critical Teaching." *College Composition and Communication* 45 (1994): 307–19.

Hohendahl, Peter. "Jürgen Habermas: The Public Sphere" *New German Critique* 1.3 (1974): 45–48.

Holub, Robert. *Jürgen Habermas: Critic in the Public Sphere.* New York: Routledge, 1991.

Hourigan, Maureen. *Literacy as Social Exchange.* Albany: State U of New York P, 1994.

Jameson, Fredric. Foreword. *The Postmodern Condition.* By Jean-François Lyotard. Trans. Geoff Bennington and Brian Massumi. Minneapolis: U of Minnesota P, 1984. vii–xxi.

———. "On Negt and Kluge." Robbins, *Phantom Public Sphere* 42–74.

Kant, Immanuel. *Critique of Practical Reasoning.* Trans. T. K. Abbott. New York: Prometheus, 1996.

Kerr, Clark. *The Great Transformation in Higher Education, 1960–1980.* Frontiers in Education Series. Albany: State U of New York P, 1988.

Killingsworth, M. Jimmie, and Jacqueline S. Palmer. *Ecospeak: Rhetoric and Environmental Politics in America.* Carbondale: Southern Illinois UP, 1992.

Kitzhaber, Albert R. "What Is English?" Working Party Paper No. 1. *Working Papers of the Dartmouth Seminar.* ERIC, 1966. ED 082 201.

Knoblauch, C. H. "Some Observations on Freire's Pedagogy of the Oppressed." *JAC* 8 (1988): 45–54.

Kuhn, Thomas. *The Structure of Scientific Revolutions.* 3rd ed. Chicago: U of Chicago P, 1996.

Lauer, Janice. "Heuristics and Composition." *College Composition and Communication* 21 (1970): 396–404.

Lefevre, Karen. *Invention as a Social Act.* Carbondale: Southern Illinois UP, 1987.

Liebman, Stuart, and Alexander Kluge. "On New German Cinema, Art, Enlightenment, and the Public Sphere—An Interview with Alexander Kluge." *October* 46 (1988): 23–59.

Lutz, William D. "Making Freshman English a Happening." *College Composition and Communication* 22 (1971): 35–38.

Macrorie, Ken. *Telling Writing.* Rochelle Park, NJ: Hayden, 1968. 47 (1996): 367–82.

McAndrew, Donald A. "Ecofeminism and the Teaching of Literacy." *College Composition and Communication* 47 (1996): 367–82.

McCarthy, Thomas. Introduction. *The Structural Transformation of the Public Sphere.* By Jürgen Habermas. Cambridge: MIT P, 1989. xi–xiv.

Merod, Jim. *The Political Responsibility of the Critic.* Ithaca: Cornell UP, 1987.

Miller, Susan. *Textual Carnivals: The Politics of Composition.* Carbondale: Southern Illinois UP, 1991.

Minter, Deborah Williams, Anne Ruggles Gere, and Deborah Keller-Cohen. "Learning Literacies." *College English* 57 (1995): 669–87.

Moffett, James. *Teaching the Universe of Discourse.* Boston: Houghton, 1968.

Murray, Donald. *A Writer Teaches Writing.* Boston: Houghton, 1968.

Myers, Greg. "Reality, Consensus, and Reform in the Rhetoric of Composition Teaching." *College English* 48 (1986): 154–73.

———. "The Social Construction of Two Biologists' Proposals." *Written Communication* 2 (1985): 219–45.

Negt, Oskar, and Alexander Kluge. *Public Sphere and Experience.* Minneapolis: U of Minnesota P, 1993.

North, Stephen M. *The Making of Knowledge in Composition: Portrait of an Emerging Field.* Portsmouth, NH: Boynton, 1987.

Ohmann, Richard. *English in America: A Radical View of the Profession.* New York: Oxford UP, 1976.

———. "Graduate Students, Professionals, Intellectuals." *College English* 52 (1990): 247–57.

Olson, Gary A. "Encountering the Other: Postcolonial Theory and Composition Scholarship." *JAC* 18 (1998): 45–56.

———. Foreword. *Teachers, Discourses, and Authority in the Postmodern Composition Classroom.* By Xin Liu Gale. Albany: State U of New York P, 1996. vii–ix.

———. "History, *Praxis,* and Change: Paulo Freire and the Politics of Literary." Olson and Gale 155–68.

———. "Toward a Post-Process Composition: Abandoning the Rhetoric of Assertion." *Post-Process Theory: Beyond the Writing-Process Paradigm.* Ed. Thomas Kent. Carbondale: Southern Illinois UP, 1999. 7–15.

Olson, Gary A., and Sidney I. Dobrin, eds. *Composition Theory for the Postmodern Classroom.* Albany: State U of New York P, 1994.

Olson, Gary A., and Lester Faigley. "Language, Politics, and Composition: A Conversation with Noam Chomsky." Olson and Gale 61–95.

Olson, Gary A., and Irene Gale, eds. *(Inter)views: Cross-Disciplinary Perspectives on Rhetoric and Literacy.* Carbondale: Southern Illinois UP, 1991.

Polan, Dana. "The Public's Fear; or, Media as Monster in Habermas, Negt, and Kluge." Robbins, *Phantom Public Sphere* 33–41.

Reynolds, John Frederick, ed. *Rhetoric, Cultural Studies, and Literacy.* Hillsdale: Erlbaum, 1995.

Robbins, Bruce, ed. *Cosmopolitics: Thinking and Feeling Beyond the Nation.* Minneapolis: U of Minnesota P, 1998.

———. *Intellectuals: Aesthetics, Politics, Academics.* Minneapolis: U of Minnesota P, 1990.

———, ed. *The Phantom Public Sphere.* Minneapolis: U of Minnesota P, 1993.

Roberts, Patricia. "Habermas' Varieties of Communicative Action." *JAC* 11 (1991): 275–92.

Rorty, Richard. *The Consequences of Pragmatism.* Minneapolis: U of Minnesota P, 1982.

———. *Philosophy and Social Hope.* London: Penguin, 1999.

Ross, Andrew. *No Respect: Intellectuals and Popular Culture.* New York: Routledge, 1989.

Royster, Jacqueline Jones, and Jean C. Williams. "History in the Spaces Left: African American Presence and Narratives of Composition Studies." *CCC* 50.4 (1999): 563–84.

Scholes, Robert. *Textual Power: Literary Theory and the Teaching of English.* New Haven: Yale UP, 1985.

Schutz, Aaron, and Anne Ruggles Gere. "Service Learning and English Studies: Rethinking 'Public' Service." *College English* 60 (1998): 129–49.

Sebberson, David. "Composition, Philosophy, and Rhetoric: The Problem of Power." *JAC* 13 (1993): 199–216.

Sennett, Richard. *The Fall of Public Man.* New York: Norton, 1974.

Shaughnessy, Mina. *Errors and Expectations: A Guide for the Teacher of Basic Writing.* New York: Oxford UP, 1977.

Shor, Ira. *Critical Teaching and Everyday Life.* Boston: South End, 1980.

———. "Educating the Educators: A Freirean Approach to the Crisis in Teacher Education." *Freire for the Classroom: A Sourcebook for Liberatory Teachers.* Ed. Ira Shor. Portsmouth, NH: Boynton, 1987. 7–32.

Shor, Ira, and Paulo Freire. *A Pedagogy for Liberation.* South Hadley, MA: Bergin, 1987.

———. "What Is the 'Dialogical Method' of Teaching?" *Journal of Education* 169.3 (1987): 11–31.

Spellmeyer, Kurt. *Common Ground: Dialogue, Understanding and the Teaching of Composition.* New York: Prentice Hall, 1993.

Tompkins, Jane. "Pedagogy of the Distressed." *College English* 52 (1990): 653–60.

Trimbur, John. "Consensus and Difference in Collaborative Learning." *College English* 51 (1989): 602–17.

Villanueva, Victor. "Considerations for American Freireistas." *The Politics of Writing Instruction: Postsecondary.* Ed. Richard Bullock and John Trimbur. Portsmouth, NH: Boynton, 1991: 247–62.

Waddell, Craig. *Landmark Essays on Rhetoric and the Environment.* Hillsdale: Erlbaum, 1997.

Ward, Irene. "How Democratic Can We Get? The Internet, the Public Sphere, and Public Discourse." *JAC* 17 (1997): 365–80.

Watkins, Evan. *Work Time: English Departments and the Circulation of Cultural Value.* Stanford: Stanford UP, 1989.

Weiler, Michael, and W. Barnett Pearce, eds. *Public Discourse in America.* Tuscaloosa: U of Alabama P, 1992.

Welch, Nancy. "Worlds in the Making: The Literacy Project as Potential Space." *JAC* 16 (1996): 61–80.

Wells, Susan. *The Dialectics of Representation.* Baltimore: Johns Hopkins UP, 1985.

———. "Habermas, Communicative Competence, and the Teaching of Technical Discourse." *Theory in the Classroom.* Ed. Cary Nelson. Urbana: U of Illinois P, 1986. 245–69.

———. "Rogue Cops and Health Care: What Do We Want from Public Writing?" *College Composition and Communication* 47 (1996): 325–41.

———. *Sweet Reason: Intersubjective Rhetoric and the Discourses of Modernity.* Chicago: U of Chicago P, 1996.

Williams, Raymond. *Keywords: A Vocabulary of Culture and Society.* New York: Oxford UP, 1985.

Yancy, Kathleen Blake, and Michael Spooner. "Collaboration, Cooperation, and the Writing Self." *College Composition and Communication* 49 (1998): 45–62.

Young, Richard. "Paradigms and Problems: Needed Research in Rhetorical Invention." *Research in Composing.* Ed. Charles Cooper and Lee Odell. Urbana: NCTE, 1978. 29–47.

INDEX

CHRISTIAN R. WEISSER is an assistant professor of English at the University of Hawaii (Hilo). He is a faculty advisor for the UH Hilo Service-Learning Program and the coordinator of Distance Education in English at UH Hilo. He has edited and co-authored several books about writing, including *Ecocomposition: Theoretical and Pedagogical Perspectives, Natural Discourse: Toward Ecocomposition,* and *Electronic Theses and Dissertations: A Sourcebook for Educators, Students, and Librarians.*